God bless you

love

[signature]

Praise for *A Visit from Heaven*:

"Our Lady's message is as important and urgent today as it was when she first spoke to the children in Kibeho in the 1980's. She begs us to repent and turn in love to her Son. Thanks to Immaculée for reminding us of Mary's loving and hope-filled message to the world. This heavenly conversation will renew your faith and your love for God and Our Lady."

Rev. Tim Farrell

"For years my struggle with worldly attachments stood in the way of a deeper relationship with Jesus. As I grew in my love for Our Lady, particularly through reflecting on her messages from Kibeho and praying the Seven Sorrows Rosary, I have experienced a true conversion of heart and deeper sense of peace than I ever thought possible. Mary is a loving Mother who challenged me to walk ever closer to the Lord, all the while providing the necessary grace to do so. This book is the kind you will come back to again and again. The tender love of Mary is what everyone needs to feel to renew their strength and vigor in their faith."

Mr. Tom Korta

"As a priest I desire in a special way to come to Mary as my mother. From the time she stood at the cross with her Son in His last moments, Jesus revealed that she is our Mother, "Woman behold your son, son behold your mother." I have witnessed personally the love that Immaculée has for Mary and her ardent desire to share the messages of Our Lady of Kibeho with all the world. I've also experienced countless others that she has drawn closer to Mary, including myself. Immaculée has helped me know this loving Mother in a special way as a priest. I believe that she will continue to draw others to Mary through her books, retreats, and lectures. This is book is one you will never forget."

Fr. Michael J. Denk

"Immaculée Ilibagiza understands the immense love of Our Blessed Mother and has been graced with the gift to share this knowledge. The messages brought to us in "A Visit from Heaven", along with her personal reflections, truly bring light to the urgent call of Our Blessed Mother to return to her Son through prayer, sincere devotion to the Rosary, and the Sacraments of Reconciliation and the Eucharist. When you read this book, you will feel blessed to know Our Lady of Kibeho and will come away knowing that you are truly loved and that GOD IS REAL. Thank you Immaculée, you give humanity a glimmer of hope!"

The team at My Saint My Hero
Amy, Antonija, Christine, & Jackie

"I am forever grateful to Immaculée for introducing me to Our Lady of Kibeho, Mother of the Word. To experience this heavenly conversation, where Immaculée adds her comments explaining the meaning of the Rwandan culture behind the interactions between Our Lady and Alphonsine, is really a treasure! As a convert to Catholicism, I did not have a strong connection to the Virgin Mary and so it is with a joyful heart that I now know I have a heavenly Mother who loves me with a warm and tender heart. As Immaculée shares more and more of these beautiful and heartfelt Heavenly conversations from Kibeho we can experience the intense love that Our Lady has for each one of us."

Mrs. Kathy Lesnar

Unsuspectingly and providentially, God led me to Immaculée Ilibagiza and through her to Our Lady of Kibeho. Immaculée's faith and prayers allowed her to forgive when most would find it virtually impossible. In turn, she inspires me and others to such love and faith. Her love for Christ and for Mary, His most loving Mother, is part of the very fabric of her being. In Kibeho, Rwanda, Mary appeared to young people asking them to plead with God's people to give their lives and hearts to her Son. The Mother of the Word calls all of us to prayer, love, forgiveness and healing; to be brothers and sisters in Christ. Part of Immaculée's story is her mission to continue to spread the message of Mary at Kibeho. Immaculée has shown many that not only is that message real, it is possible. When I read this book I realized that my life and priesthood had been renewed through Our Lady of Kibeho. Thank you Immaculée! Thank you Blessed Virgin Mary! Thank you Jesus!   *Fr. Jim Meysenburg*

"The words of Our Lady of Kibeho speaks to a world so desperate in need of faith, hope and love and this book is like water in an oasis."
                    Fr. José Lizardo Morales

"The message of Kibeho calls us to repentance as we work to establish God's kingdom, a kingdom of justice and peace."
                    Fr. James Francis Callahan

How grateful I am to have to come to know Our Lady of Kibeho through Immaculée! This is such a great grace that one cannot thank Our Lord enough. There is not enough space to say all I wish to say, but I would encourage and even implore you to give Our Lady a chance in your life. She has changed mine in a profound way. She is truly a Mother and has brought me back to her Son, Jesus, and into the Catholic Church. No matter who you are or where you have been, Our Lady loves you for you are her child and God's child! I am so thankful that Immaculée is sharing her story and spreading Our Lady's message from Kibeho, which is so important and is meant for the whole world. I have been blessed to have been to Kibeho and I encourage everyone, if you are able, to make a pilgrimage there with Immaculée, for in seeking Our Lady you will draw closer to God and His love for you.   *Mr. Greg Amaya*

A Visit From Heaven

A Visit From Heaven

The Last Apparition of Our Lady in Kibeho, Rwanda

by
Immaculée Ilibagiza

www.immaculee.com

Published by Immaculée Ilibagiza
P.O Box 4075
New York, NY 10163

ISBN: 978-1-4507-4298-6
Price: $18.95

Cover Design by Kathy Lesnar
Photograph by Michael Collapy
Page layout by Jill Voges

1st Edition, November 2010

This book is dedicated to Our Lady Of Kibeho,
Mary the Mother of mankind, for your love and perseverance.
Happy Feast Dear Mother! May the whole world come to know
and love you, who have given us the Savior, and may everyone
come to know the love you hold for each one of us.

Contents

Foreword

I am only good at a few things. I can't fix a faucet. I would stink at selling cars, used ones particularly. I can't write a poem. But, the few things I know how to do, I do to the best of my ability. So far it has worked out. First, I work hard at being a good husband, then a good dad. Lastly, I make movies. Sometimes they are good. Like my kids, sometimes they are great. None of these three would I do well without a tremendous faith in God, a faith that was learned, a faith that was earned. It did not appear. It came with effort. But, over the years, especially through the production of *"The Passion Of The Christ,"* I witnessed faith in a different way. I witnessed faith put into action, both in my own life and in the world. It is an active faith that the world needs today, and it is that active faith I have seen at work in Immaculée Ilibagiza as she shares her testimony and encourages others to discover their faith and put it into action. I had imagined Immaculée's heart through reading her best selling book, *"Left To Tell."* I have since embraced her soul as we struggle to make that best seller into a movie worthy of its printed word. Through that process, I have been blessed to learn more about what really motivates her in life and what is behind her passion to write this latest book.

I am inspired by Immaculée's efforts to share this treasure with the world. The apparitions of Our Lady of Kibeho are one of a kind. We have heard of Mary appearing to children all over the world, but the apparitions in Kibeho have very distinct graces. There, Our Lady came and talked with the children for hours at a time and took into account the culture of the beautiful country of Rwanda. Our Lady became a friend of the children in Kibeho, danced with them, taught them songs, and reminded them how much her Son loves each one of His children in the world. In this book, *"A Visit from Heaven,"* you will feel like you've been given the chance to glimpse heaven!

In her account of how faith sustained her in her New York Times Best Seller, *"Left To Tell,"* Immaculée described her childhood, her separation from her family members and their tragic deaths. She tells the story of how her father's parting gift of a rosary became her refuge and armor while hiding with seven other women for three months in a tiny bathroom, being hunted by Hutu militia. I always wondered how Immaculée could have so much faith? Where did she get it? It was when I read her third book, "Our Lady of Kibeho", that I understood the origin of her strength. She came from a faith-filled family that taught her by example to trust God and to love one another. In that book, we learn that Our Lady tried to warn of the impending Rwandan genocide of 1994 that killed almost a million people and left thousands misplaced and orphaned, and even more brokenhearted.

Rwanda is an example to the world and we need to learn from what happened there. As Our Lady once said in Kibeho, *"If I am coming here it does not mean that my message is only for Rwanda, nor just Africa, but for the entire world."* In today's age of disobedience, we have to work so hard just to maintain even minimum momentum in the direction toward heaven. Perhaps this is why Our Mother is coming over and over around the world. Perhaps in today's world hell has made earth home, allowing heaven no choice but to intervene. I believe

Immaculée survived the physical as well as the supernatural warfare in Rwanda to witness that Mary so desperately wants us to stay on the one true path that leads to heaven through the understanding that we are so deeply loved by her Son, Our Lord, Jesus Christ.

Immaculée Ilibagiza understands the urgency of the hour, and it is so apparent through her writings and reflections. After reading this book, your heart will be touched with the beloved words of Our Blessed Mother and the seeds of your faith will grow roots. May your curiosity lead you to Our Blessed Mother as she continues to appear around the world and may your heart, like mine, be forever changed by the Love of her Son, Jesus Christ.

Our Blessed Mother is inviting you to come with her on the path to heaven. I hope you accept the invitation...

Steve McEveety
Producer of The Passion of the Christ

Preface

Immaculée Ilibagiza's passion, her God-given mission, is witnessing to the world on behalf of Our Lady of Kibeho. As our Heavenly Mother has said, her messages in Kibeho are not just for that village or for Rwanda or for Africa but for the entire world. Immaculée intends to make sure the whole world hears those messages!

Those of us who met Immaculée in *Left to Tell* learned of her devotion to Our Lady in the rosary: the prayer she recited again and again each day, asking Mary to intercede with Jesus on her behalf. In her second book, *Led by Faith*, we learn of the apparitions of Our Lady in Kibeho and the deepening relationship between Mother Mary and Immaculée in the years just preceding the genocide.

Immaculée's next two books, *Our Lady of Kibeho* and *If Only We Had Listened*, show in even greater depth Immaculée's devotion to her heavenly Mother. In *Our Lady of Kibeho* we meet the three visionaries whose apparitions were recognized by the Vatican in 2001. We are also introduced to five other visionaries who received messages from Mary and/or Jesus. *If Only We Had Listened* contains many of the messages received at Kibeho: messages revealing Our Lady's great desire that her children pray to her through the Rosary of Seven Sorrows and expressing her warnings about the traps satan lays for those who stray from the path of her Son.

A Visit from Heaven is set in Kibeho on November 28, 1989. Here we meet Alphonsine Mumureke who, as a 16 year old high school student, met Our Lady on that date nine years before. Alphonsine is experiencing a mixture of joyful anticipation and heartfelt sorrow. Immaculée is our guide as we draw close to the visionary who is about to see her Heavenly Mother, face-to-face, for the final time this side of eternity. Using tape recordings, writings and interviews of those present that day, Immaculée describes the setting and the bittersweet atmosphere of this emotional goodbye. She's able to translate not just the words of the beautiful exchange between Our Lady and Alphonsine from Kinyarwanda but, more importantly, the nuanced Rwandan cultural meanings in those exchanges.

It's like listening to one side of a telephone conversation, except when Our Lady asks that her words be repeated. Otherwise what Mary said has to be inferred from the visionary's response.

After each quote, Immaculée comments - perhaps providing background from previous visions or offering thanks and praise for the great gentleness and love of Our Lady or explaining what's not evident to those not immersed in the culture. For example, Immaculée tells us that when Alphonsine freely expresses her emotions to Mary, *"It's a sign of great trust and love between mother and daughter...Rwandans are much more reserved by nature and don't show feelings...for those words to be said, it can only come from a child who feels truly loved unconditionally."*

Through the commentary we come to understand that Our Lady revels in the innocence of all her Kibeho visionaries. She has asked them to sing and dance for her. They have sometimes called her sweetheart and darling. Mary's been accused of spoiling them. Her reply is, *"Blessed is the one who has somebody who spoils them, who cherishes them."* Those of us who have been called spoiled can draw great consolation from Mary's words!

In this lovely little book, Immaculée is able to give us a deep sense of the depth and breadth of the marvelous love our Heavenly Mother has for each one of us. It's a powerful reminder that each of us is created in the image and likeness of our loving God.

Father John McHale
Pastor St. Patrick Parish
White Haven, Pennsylvania

A Note from the Author

Dear Friend,

I call you a friend, because if you are reading this book, we have a lot to share in these pages; feelings, emotions, laugher and tears. I am grateful that you have it in your hands, maybe by accident or by the love of God and Our Lady, or maybe just because a friend referred it to you, or gave it to you as a gift, or maybe because you have read my other books and were inspired. Whatever reason led you to this book, I thank God, because I think it is the most important work I have done. I want every human being to know that they have a Mother, and what is more important, is to help you really get to know her, how she talks, what makes her happy and how much she loves you. That is what led me to share this last conversation between Our Lady and Alphonsine. I also want to thank you and welcome you with open arms to take this beautiful journey with me. My prayer is that at the end of this book, you will know without a shadow of doubt that God is real and He cares for and loves you.

I am from Rwanda, a tiny country in Africa. I survived the horrible genocide that took place there in 1994. I survived by hiding in a cramped bathroom of 3 by 4 feet with seven other women. We stayed there for 3 months in silence, being haunted by the killers that were ordered by the government in place at the time to kill the entire Tutsi tribe my family and I belonged to. I survived, but the rest of my family I left behind when I went into hiding didn't. Though I am alive, the true survival was not of the machetes and guns, rather it was of the monsters of anger and hate that ate away at my peace and my whole being. Through the prayer of the rosary my father gave me when we were separating, that I said daily from morning until night, I found a way to forgive and to let go of the anger. I shared this story at length in my first book *Left To Tell,* and its sequel, *Led By Faith.*

However, the subject of this book is not the story of the genocide, but of the apparitions of Our Lady of Kibeho. I have written two books about this subject, the first being the history of the apparitions in *Our Lady of Kibeho* and the second about the actual messages in *If Only We Had Listened.* The messages that were approved date from 1981 to 1989, but only a few of these messages have been published and Our Lady wishes for these messages to reach all her children in the world. In Rwanda, if we had paid attention to these messages, we could have prevented the genocide! She also made it clear that these messages did not only concern Rwanda, nor Africa alone, but the whole world. In this book, I not only share with you the full account of the last apparition to the visionary, Alphonsine, but I have added my own comments and personal reflections. I have done this with the hope that it will help you to better understand the full meaning of the messages and some of the words and phrases used as they were shared in my native language, Kinyarwanda.

This last conversation between Our Lady and Alphonsine is not of this world. It is a rare jewel, a blessing from God to the world, between a heavenly being and one of the earth. I don't know about you, but for me the thought of it alone, that we have these words coming from heaven today directly to us, confirming our faith and the messages of the bible, reconfirming what was told two thousand years ago, takes my breath away. They make me feel so lucky to even have this occasion in my lifetime. It feels like we are living in the time of the first disciples. Many people have left their faith because a certain priest, pastor, church leader, or some other person of faith did something wrong or hurt them in some way. It made them question everything they had ever learned about their faith. However, Our Lady's messages remind us that Heaven is real, Purgatory is real, Hell is real and that matters of faith are between individuals and God. We are instruments to each other and if an instrument fails God we need to pray for him. Don't risk losing heaven because of another human being! Our Lady reminds us that in the first place we should seek to please God, not human eyes. We must lend each other prayer without losing our faith, because we are taking this journey together.

God Bless,
Immaculée

Introduction

The apparitions of Our Lady in Rwanda began on November 28, 1981 to a high school student named Alphonsine Mumureke. Our Lady's first visit to Alphosine came at about 12:35 p.m. when the students were finishing their lunch. It was Alphonsine's turn to clean the dishes that day as the students took turns doing each week. While putting away dishes, she suddenly lost sight of the world she was in and found herself somewhere else much more beautiful, in a valley that had the most beautiful grass and no trees. She then saw a beautiful lady emerging from a white cloud surrounded by a light brighter than the sun, but gentle to the eyes, which made it easy to look at her. She was dressed all in white, wearing a white dress and white veil. She was more beautiful that anyone Alphonsine had ever seen in her life. The beautiful lady then beckoned Alphonsine in the most tender voice:

"My child?"

Alphonsine answered:

"Karame."

Meaning, *"Long life to you,"* a polite way of answering somebody who calls you in Rwandan culture.

Alphonsine then asked:

"Who are you my Lady?"

And the Lady replied:

Alphonsine during an apparition, like a child smiling to Our Lady in the very beginning of the apparition, 1981.

"I am the Mother of the Word."

As the dialogue continued, the Lady asked:

"What do you esteem the most in your life?"

Alphonsine answered:

"I love God and His Mother who gave birth to the Redeemer."

The Lady said in amazement:

"Is that true?"

Alphonsine said:

"Yes, it's true."

Then the Lady declared:

"If that is the case, I came to console you, because I heard your prayers. I want your friends to have more faith, because they don't have enough."

And then Alphonsine said:

"If it is you, the Mother of God, who is coming to remind us here in our school that we don't have enough faith, then you truly love us and I thank you for that."

Our Lady then said good-bye to her and rose until she disappeared into the sky. When Alphonsine lost sight of her, she suddenly collapsed onto the ground in a state of semi-consciousness as her schoolmates and teachers gathered around her and demanded to know what had happened. Alphonsine confided that she had seen and spoken with the Virgin, that the Lady's beauty was so great it could not be described in words, and that the golden light radiating from the Blessed Mother was filled with the immeasurable love Mary felt for all the people in the world, whom she called her "earthly children."

As happened many years before and thousands of miles away with Bernadette of Lourdes and the three young visionaries to whom the Virgin appeared in Fatima, Alphonsine's apparition of the Blessed Mother was not believed and the poor girl was dismissed as a liar and was cruelly ridiculed and mocked. But the Blessed Mother continued to appear to Alphonsine with messages of love that she instructed the young visionary to share with her classmates. Facing even greater persecution, accusations of heresy and threats of expulsion from school, Alphonsine prayed for the Virgin to appear to other students so people would believe what she said was true. The Virgin answered Alphonsine's prayers and soon Mary appeared to two other girls at Kibeho High School, Marie-Clare, one of Alphonsine's most outspoken tormentors, and Anathalie, a respected and pious girl who was believed to always speak the truth.

Soon hundreds of local peasants began milling about the school each day waiting for the Virgin to appear to one of the girls with messages from heaven. Within weeks the entire country was talking about the three visionaries and the "Miracle of Kibeho." Reports of mystical visions in the sky above Kibeho were being broadcast on Rwandan radio as well as a miraculous rain that fell on even the sunniest days on the crowds that gathered near the school, a rain that healed the sick and cured the maimed. Soon tens of thousands of Rwandans were travelling hundreds of miles on foot to make the pilgrimage to Kibeho. Other young people also began receiving visions from the Blessed Virgin and a few were even blessed by receiving apparitions of Jesus.

The Church was alarmed by the massive crowds assembling at Kibeho and worried the miracles could be the work of the devil. The local bishop quickly launched an official investigation to scrutinize the apparitions, assembling a team of scientists, doctors, psychiatrists and theologians who subjected the visionaries to months of rigorous physical and psychological testing. The Vatican was contacted and experts were flown in from around the world to observe the states of "ecstasy" the visionaries entered during the apparitions. Needles were stuck into the visionaries during their apparitions, burning candles were held against their skin and bright lights were shone directly into their eyes, but none of the visionaries showed any reaction to physical pain inflicted upon them while conversing with the Blessed Mother. In fact, each visionary reported that when the Virgin appeared before them the crowds vanished from their view and the only thing they could see was Mary hovering above an endless field of beautiful flowers.

The scientists and an army of journalists began recording the messages the visionaries delivered from heaven. Many more medical tests and intense interrogations of the young seers were conducted in an effort to disprove true miracles were actually taking place in Kibeho. However, despite their combined investigations, the scientists and theologians found it impossible to deny that supernatural events were taking place.

The messages the visionaries delivered between 1981 and 1989 were often very similar in nature. They called for each of us to pray regularly, fill our hearts with love, avoid evil deeds and the snares of sin laid by the devil to lead us away from

God's light, to call upon the Blessed Mother to help us find the way to Jesus' love and forgiveness, and to embrace Christ's love to achieve eternal life in paradise with our Heavenly Father.

The visions were often joyous occasions during which the Blessed Mother would encourage the visionaries to lead the multitude of pilgrims in prayer, song and dances that celebrated the love of the Lord. But on one ominous day in 1982 all of the visionaries reported horrid visions of unspeakable violence, bloodshed, torture, destruction and thousands of dismembered corpses littering the landscape. It was a prophetic warning from the Virgin Mary that if Rwandans did not cleanse their hearts of hatred and fill their souls with Christ's love, evil would win out and a genocide would sweep across the land. Sadly, the Virgin's warning went unheeded and in 1994 Our Lady's prediction became reality; the terrible Rwandan genocide unfolded exactly as she prophesized.

During that dark time, the miracles of Kibeho were lost to the world and Rwanda suffered horribly in the aftermath of the holocaust. But slowly, as the years passed and the country began to heal, pilgrims began to return to Kibeho. At first it was only a trickle of the faithful seeking solace from their Heavenly Mother after losing their homes, their hope and so many of their loved ones during the war. But soon hundreds and then thousands of Rwandans began journeying to Kibeho. Rwandans from each tribe and every walk of life found that Kibeho was a place they could find forgiveness and pray together for reconciliation. Before long they were joined by pilgrims from every country in Africa and many who traveled from as far away as Europe and America. The voice of Mary was not silenced by the deeds of evil men and her love has risen above Kibeho as a beacon to the world, a signal from heaven that even in a place where darkness once held sway, God's light can always break through and touch even the most hardened or broken hearted.

Today Kibeho is being reborn and rebuilt as a holy site and millions of pilgrims are flocking to pray at the newly constructed church and shrine honoring Our Lady of Kibeho. New guest houses are being built everyday to accommodate the ever-growing number of pilgrims, many of whom regularly

The first 3 visionaries back in 1982, during an interview, from left, Anathalie, Marie Claire, Alphonsine.

The multitude of people who showed up at the apparitions in the beginning.

report seeing visions of Mary and Jesus in the sky above the village. Dozens of pilgrims say they have been miraculously cured of serious diseases while praying at the blessed site.

Kibeho, a once unknown village in one of the most remote parts of the world, is now the most visited location in Rwanda. The world's largest bronze statue of Jesus' Divine Mercy towers high on a hill above Kibeho beckoning the faithful to remember and remain true to the words and messages delivered by the Blessed Mother in this sacred place.

In 2001, after a twenty-year investigation into the events of Kibeho, the Vatican formally recognized the authenticity of the Virgin Mary's appearance to the original three visionaries; Alphonsine, Marie-Clare, and Anathalie. Kibeho has now become the only Vatican-approved Marian site on the African continent, placing the humble village on the same spiritual level with the very few officially recognized apparition sites in the world, such as Lourdes and Fatima.

The podium that was built outside in the open place.

The Dormitory

The second apparition happened the very next day after the first one, but this time Our Lady came into the dormitory where the students slept. It was here that she would appear to Alphonsine for the next nine years. Many people asked themselves, why in the dormitory? I don't know about other places, but in the Rwandan culture a bedroom is always a very respectful and private place, especially the bedroom of parents. You might spend a year in a person's home in Rwanda and never see the bedroom of the parents. It is not that anyone would prevent you, but just out of respect you would not go there, for it is considered a private and sacred place. My uncle used to tell me that the bedroom of your parents is where the parents and God create children. It is sacred and definitely not a place shared with others. The bedrooms of children are also very respected and considered private. It is generally only mothers and siblings who enter there; even fathers don't go to the bedroom of their children, unless the child is sick. Most of the time, the father will stand at the door while mothers are often welcome to go into their children's rooms to make sure they are sleeping well, to see if they are okay, or to talk to them about something they want to advise them on. It is considered a secure place where a child can talk to their mother openly and comfortably, without worry of being overheard. The bedroom is a place where you feel free to cry and where a child can share a secret with their mom.

Our Lady coming into the sleeping place of her daughters was a great message for the world. She wanted once more to

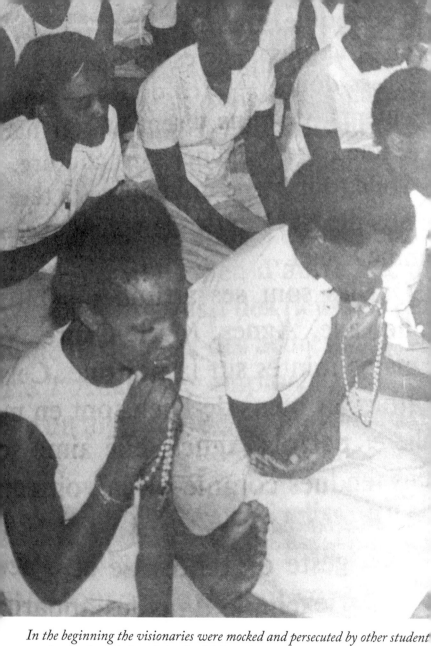

In the beginning the visionaries were mocked and persecuted by other student but in the end the whole school believed in Our Lady and joined them.

show us who she was for each one of us, a Mother. She wants to have that motherly relationship with you. She wants you to trust her, to come to talk to her with an open heart and feel the undivided attention she is giving you.

As many people were now coming to Kibeho to witness the apparitions, the school moved the place of the public apparitions outside into the open air, where a podium had been built for the visionaries to stand on while talking to Our Lady. Thousands of people would gather all day, singing, dancing and praying together, waiting for Our Lady. Many did this with no chairs to sit on, but their excitement and love for Our Lady enabled them to stand for hours on end.

Alphonsine has grown up and ready to say bye to Our Lady against her will, only because it is the will of God.

The Final Visit

After nine years of Our Lady appearing to Alphonsine, the final meeting with Our Lady would last about an hour and one-half with the crowd swelling to more than 30 thousand people to witness this final apparition. A year before, Our Lady had told Alphonsine that this would be the last time she would appear to her. Alphonsine's heart was broken and she cried a great deal during the year while she anxiously waited for her last encounter with Our Lady on November 28, 1989. Those precious hours spent with Our Lady seemed to be everything for her, as it would be very hard to say goodbye to her Heavenly Mother. She once said, "*After you have seen Mary in person and felt her indescribable love, it would be much easier to die than to be separated from this love.*" Many times I have asked the visionaries "*Who is Our Lady? What is it you love so much about her that you are willing to do anything for her, sacrificing all for her, including renouncing everything you love on earth? What is it that we do not understand?*" In response the visionaries answered, "*When you see Our Lady and you talk to her, you know she loves you more than your earthly mother. When you are in her presence there is a fullness of joy, all the joy you ever wanted to have is wrapped in her presence. It is not something you can express with words, it is heavenly.*"

I have been blessed to be present many times in Kibeho during the apparitions, but I was not present for this final conversation. However, I am so grateful to have acquired the dialogue of the entire apparition as it happened, from tape recordings, writings and interviews with those who were present. It is my joy to share this treasure with you. Like those who were there, you can only hear one side of the conversation as if you were listening to somebody talking on the telephone, but you can imagine what Our Lady might have said by how Alphonsine responded. In her love and kindness, Our Blessed Mother would sometimes ask the visionary to repeat out loud what she said to her. Alphonsine always did so out of obedience even though she didn't understand why Our Lady requested this, because during the apparitions she could not see the other people around her, only Our Lady. On some occasions she would ask Our Lady, "*Mother why are you asking me to repeat? There is only me and you here?*" and after a pause, onlookers would hear the visionary respond to what she was told saying, "*I know, I promised to be your instrument, whatever you ask of me Mother.*" It reminds me of how many times we question God on things we shouldn't, and yet we are so blind as to ask, why? Believing in Him is to trust totally because He knows better and He is Almighty.

The first part of the last apparition happened in private in the room that was once the dormitory, which had been converted into a chapel years before in honor of Our Lady. The longer part of the apparition took place later in the day on the podium outside in front of thousands of people. It is amazing that although no one was managing this heavenly event or publicizing it, it always seemed to be organized and managed like somebody had been planning it for years. The enthusiasm of those present, waiting for hours, would move one's heart. Despite many of them being poor, they would happily wash what few clothes they had to prepare themselves to be in the presence of Our Lady. Despite their material poverty, many of them would spend their savings to buy one new outfit to look their best for the apparition of the Queen of Heaven. No sacrifice was too great to make for this heavenly meeting! Most people there always made sure to wear white and blue as these were the colors of Our Lady. The dirt roads to the apparition site were rugged and dusty, which would cause their white clothes to become gray and dingy, but despite this, their souls remained bright and filled with joy as they had all come to meet Our Lady and nothing could steal this elation from them.

The whole apparition was very emotional. It didn't contain as many laughs as in the past, but brought tears instead. It was an adieu between a mother and daughter, between two people who love to be together and who love each other dearly, not wanting to part. Our Lady gave us a summary of her messages throughout the nine years. Just like any good mother, she repeats herself reminding us of the most important lessons she gave us, not for Alphonsine alone, but for the whole world. Most importantly she told us once again that we are never alone and reminded us of her great love for us. Even if we don't see her, she is there for us, always ready to intercede for us.

This reminds me that in one apparition, Jesus, encouraging us to know what kind of mother we have, explained that He created His Mother's heart only with Mercy and Love, and that His heart is full of Mercy and Love, but also of Justice. He said *"If you come to me, you will be happy with my Love and Mercy, but you will also have to face my Justice. Blessed are those who will go through my mother because she doesn't know Justice; she welcomes everyone only with Mercy and Love. When she intercedes for anyone, you get what you want because I don't know how to say no to my mother."*

In this book, sometimes you might not understand fully why Alphonsine responded a certain way, but when that happens, I tell myself that maybe it was not meant for me and I pray for discernment and wisdom to understand what is mine. I suggest you do the same as you read these messages. However, in God's infinite wisdom, the conversation was done in a way that will allow you to learn and understand so much even only listening to one side of the conversation. You will also learn from the songs which were requested by Our Lady. They are full of lessons and words Our Lady is giving us.

Alphonsine during the apparition, her face suddenly becomes sad. There were investigators, doctors and theologians hired by the church who checked every step of the apparition to prove it's authenticity.

How it Started on November 28, 1989

As was the custom on the day of the apparition, Alphonsine and a number of guests and school leaders waited in prayer in the small dormitory chapel. Alphonsine was wearing her usual khaki skirt and white shirt with her hair combed back, reflecting her simplicity and modesty. Her rosary was clasped gently in her hands as she prayed with all those present. Exactly at 12:35 p.m., she suddenly fell to her knees on the cement floor, which seemed to happen through an unseen force. The sound echoed through the room, but there was no sound of pain from Alphonsine. Turning her head in one direction, as if someone called her name, she looked with a radiant smile to somebody who seemed to be in the air a few meters above the floor. Her face became transfigured and reflected an emotion of deep love, which was directed toward the one she was seeing. Her mannerisms conveyed a deep respect as she took a deep breath and opened her arms and raised her hands towards heaven. The person she looked up to seemed to be standing approximately three meters above the ground, and in close proximity to her. It could be seen by all those present that her gaze was not one that peered at the ceiling or into infinity, but it was evident she was looking at something fixed right in front of her as her eyes were riveted. Her fellow students stood around her in amazement and watched.

A number of journalists from all over the world, especially

from Europe and Africa, were positioning themselves around her to capture the moment with cameras and record what she was saying. As the journalists scurried to take pictures and record her voice, Alphonsine was oblivious to anything that was going on around her. Those in charge of the investigation on behalf of the Church were also busying themselves around her, taking pictures with bright flashes right in front of her face, which would blind anyone or at the very least cause a reaction, but there was no response, nothing! They began to try and pull her purse from her and tried to move her hands, but without success. In the midst of all this commotion, her face emitted a gentleness, a peaceful smile undisturbed and unaware of anything or anyone that was around her, except that which her eyes beheld in front of her. Suddenly the crowd became hushed as Alphonsine began to speak; welcoming the one she was looking at, she began with a native song:

"Kundwa, kundwa, kundwa Mariya…Be loved, be loved, be loved Mary…"

She then paused and, seeming to respond to what was spoken to her, she said:

"I am aware of that, I didn't think about it much because I know it is supposed to be like that and it has been a year since I knew about it. This morning I passed by there and I felt a great sadness just to think that I will never be kneeling there again waiting for you. I will get used to it as you told me. Even in normal life, when a friend comes to visit you and they leave, you feel sad."

From Alphonsine's response to Our Lady, we can determine that she must have asked Alphonsine about how she felt about this being her last visit. The place Alphonsine mentioned passing by is the podium where the visionaries stood while having the apparitions. It is important to give a brief reflection on Alphonsine's response to Our Lady, in which she stated that even in normal life when somebody comes to visit you and says good-bye, you feel sad. In the Rwandan culture there is a great sense of accommodation. There is an ancient proverb in Rwanda that says, "*A Guest is a King*" therefore you must treat a guest with attention and love. When I was young, I remember when I knew my friends were going to come and visit me I would begin preparing for days in anticipation of their visit. It became a family affair in which everyone got involved. My mom and dad would ask me what I kind of food and drinks they needed to get. They would also give me money to go and buy something special for them. I have experienced this great sadness many times when someone comes to visit and then has to leave. I believe it's because you look forward to their visit so much. When they came they would stay for many hours, that is expected in the Rwandan culture. In fact it is not unusual for them to stay for a half day, all day, or even up to three days. In Kibeho, not only did Our Lady stay hours longer than any other apparition in the history of Marian apparitions, but before leaving she would find a reason to start saying goodbye about an hour before as we do in Rwanda. As a gesture of her love and thoughtfulness for her children and our culture, she acted in the same way that we do when we have guests. Knowing we desired her to stay a bit longer, Our Lady prepared us well in advance that she was about to leave, enabling us to enjoy her company as a guest a bit longer. Oh, how good and gracious a Mother she is!

I remember one time Our Lady said to the visionary that she was about to leave almost two hours before she left, and then the visionary said, "*Oh Mother, you have been here for only 10 minutes, how can you leave so quickly? Don't you see it has been such a long time we did not see each other, I missed you?"* In the Rwandan culture, if you have spent five hours as a guest it is not unusual that your host will say such a thing, and that is how we all feel when you really are enjoying a friend's visit. To this Our Lady replied with the precise time, as people heard the visionary repeating, *"It is 5:12 p.m.? It cannot be an hour and 12 minutes already. It feels like you just came and said hi and now you are saying that you are leaving already!"* Our Lady had started appearing to her at 4:00 p.m. It was a confirmation to all those present that Our Lady was truly appearing, since from the time the apparition began the visionary's head and eyes had been directed heavenward. She did not have a watch on and could not have known the exact time. Our Lady must have told her what time it was and it was indeed another sign of Our Lady's presence among us. Apparitions can be overwhelmingly beautiful, filling up one's soul with a sense of peace. However, it can be challenging for some to believe, as those who are watching don't see anything other than hearing one side of the conversation. They might ask, "What if the visionaries are making it up? What if no one is really there?" To experience the joy of an apparition, for it to make sense, you must believe that they are seeing somebody. You have to be willing to hear with the ears of the heart and see with the eyes of the heart. Like all gifts, we must be willing to accept them.

Alphonsine then became silent as though she was listening and then she answered in tears saying:

"No."

And she continued to listen intently while looking at Our Lady and then she said:

"Yes, I am ready and I am grateful that you prepared me well during this last year. Somehow I found unusual strength to accept this separation as I kept thinking that I will never look forward to our meeting again or be able to talk to you in person, and to cry to you when I need you. I will only meet you in prayer like everyone else from now on."

> Those who knew Alphonsine said that she was in terrible pain when Our Lady told her that she would only come back once more. It was also stated that after she had said goodbye, Alphonsine was sick for awhile, deeply saddened, lonely and in tears. Even if she continued to see her sometimes in private, the private times are shorter and rare and unannounced. When Our Lady says goodbye, she knows how much these children have come to know of her love for them, unlike many of us who are still blind to it. Although she leaves the visionary in a visible sense, she promises to be with them always even if they can't see her with their bodily eyes. Although the separation is difficult for the visionary, Our Lady is ever encouraging and assuring them of her motherly love. Anathalie, who still lives in Kibeho today, told me, *"Seeing Our Lady and living without seeing her, is a cross I have to carry for the rest of my life. Like other sufferings I have to endure, I miss her every day, but when it becomes unbearable sometimes I feel her presence so closely. I can't explain it, it is heavenly. She never leaves us."*

These words of Alphonsine, "*I will only meet you in prayer like everyone else from now on*" are also a comfort for me. They remind me that I too meet Our Lady as well, when I pray and talk to her. We all meet her when we invoke her in prayer.

She then listened and said:

"*Yes, yes.*"

She then repeated what she was told at the same time asking:

"*You mean at 4:00 p.m.?*"

And then she said:

"*No, I know you will always be at my side even if I will not see you with my eyes. I have complete trust in you. And you are right, this separation will give me a chance to always reflect on the good things you told me when we were together, like everybody else who heard your messages. You asked me what will I think of when I pass by that place? I know it will hurt, especially during the first days, but I think it will get better with time. In the future, if I am able to come back here, although I am not sure where life will take me after school, however even in my old age, if I get a chance to come back here, on this ground, I know I will be very happy just to be here, and if I should cry, it will be tears of joy.*"

At about the age of 14, many high school students in Rwanda who are fortunate enough to obtain a scholarship have to leave home to go to boarding school to continue their education. This is what Alphonsine did. During the school year she lived at the school. The only time she went home was to visit her parents for three months of summer vacation, two weeks during Christmas, and two weeks during Easter. The discipline at school was strict. In most boarding schools everyone had to wake up at the same hour and do the morning chores, which entailed duties such as cleaning toilets and sweeping outside. Everyone would also go to mass in total silence, go to bed at the same hour, and eat at the same time. There was no room for distraction as there was only one hour a day set aside for recreation while the other times were for study and doing your homework. In school you didn't choose what to eat, rather they had a schedule of what you would eat for the year for every meal - breakfast, lunch and dinner. Students were permitted to receive guests from outside the school, like family members, only once a month. Boarding school lasted for six years and the parents of the children were very fond of the school as they knew their children were protected. When Alphonsine told Our Lady that she didn't know where life would take her after high school, it was understood why she would state this since no one was sure unless you had a scholarship to continue in university. No one was sure how they would be able to live outside of school and be able to organize their own schedule, but somehow it always seemed to work out. You go to the school as a child and afterwards you come out an adult to face the world and all its challenges.

In a small way I know what Alphonsine must have felt like when she talks about what she will feel when she comes back to Kibeho as an adult. Even in her old age, she will always remember all that she experienced there on those sacred grounds where Our Lady visited and spoke with her. I too was there many times during Our Lady's apparitions in Kibeho. Today I live in the USA, but I still go to Rwanda two to three times a year taking pilgrims to Kibeho to share the memories and the love I have felt on that ground. I miss it so much! When I am there all the memories come flooding back to my mind of those wondrous days of being present when Our Lady came to Kibeho. It is as though I can hear the words once again spoken by Alphonsine. I feel as though I have returned to my home where I have come to visit my mom, a place where I can share everything with her that is deep within my heart without fear. It is a place that I never tire of or get enough of, and somehow I feel

like other people feel the same when they visit Kibeho.
There is something truly special on that ground and maybe
it is that way everywhere Our Lady has come to visit.

A moment of silence passed as she listened and she kept
nodding her head in agreement and saying:

"Yes… yes… uh… uh… yes…"

Then she said:

*"Last year when you told me that this would be the last time,
the first few months were very hard as it was difficult to think of
how I would be able to prepare myself for this last visit. I thought it
would be extremely hard, but somehow my heart feels accepting."*

She listened for a while and she kept saying:

"Yes… yes… yes…"

And then she said:

*"I will tell her/him so she/he will inform the others about 4:00
p.m."*

> In the Rwandan language, Kinyarwanda, when you are
> talking about someone and you don't mention their name,
> no one will know if you are talking about a man or woman
> as our language will refer to a human being but will not
> specifically differentiate genders. It is not like English when
> you refer to her or him. Alphonsine is probably talking
> about the director of the school here, who was also a nun,
> or maybe the nun who was the in charge of discipline at
> school, or the priest of the parish of Kibeho, they all were
> very involved in the apparitions but we don't know for sure.
> The apparition a year before this one was also focused on
> saying goodbye to Alphonsine. She was in tears then, and

today her eyes filled with tears as well. Anytime I read this it makes me think that I still have a long way to go before I know my Mother Mary. By her tearful response it is obvious that Alphonsine finds it very difficult to be separated from seeing Our Lady. Through the eyes and feelings of Alphonsine we too felt the same way as those who were present that day. We desire to also know Our Mother, and if this is what the visionaries feel in her presence, should we be scared to die? Should we be scared to meet our Heavenly Mother one day or should we look forward to this? And if we look forward to this, should we not do all it takes to be ready, and not to miss out on this occasion? Reflecting on this takes me back to the Bible, to what God really wants of us, to the message Our Lady is bringing us. Shouldn't we listen to her with all our heart so we can hope to share that joy? This conversation, if you think about it, can renew our faith and our love for God.

As tears filled her eyes she forced a slight smile, and tried to justify the tears that fell effortlessly to the ground saying,

"Since I am crying now, I hope I won't cry again later, but I cry so easily, I am not sure."

Like all the messages this too was given in Kinyarwanda and it is important to reflect a bit on its actual meaning in the Rwandan culture. What Alphonsine is actually saying to Our Lady when she says she hopes not to cry later, is so much more than just what you read. It is a great sign of love and trust between a mother and a daughter. These words cannot be exchanged between friends, but only between a mother and a child. Rwandans are much more reserved by nature and don't show their feelings much in that way. For those words to be said, it can only come from a child who feels truly loved unconditionally, without any fear of being judged or reproached in any way by a mother. Normally, those words would come from a child who is still so innocent at a young age. It is really a mark of an untarnished relationship between a mother and a daughter, a great confidence. Normally, like all teenagers, girls get mad at their mothers when they correct them, remind them to dress appropriately, or remind them to clean up. Often times, children will recognize when they grow up that their mother's rules were in their best interest and out of love for them. So these words spoken by Alphonsine were said by a child who felt understood by a mother at all levels and had great respect for the one to whom she addressed.

Our Lady of Kibeho sometimes was accused of spoiling the visionaries, being easy on them and cherishing them greatly, and treating them like babies. Sometimes Alphonsine was heard calling Our Lady "*Sweetheart, darling...*" and people complained that it couldn't be Our Lady appearing because she had never been addressed that way before. But remember, Kibeho is also the first place Our Lady had conversations for hours with the visionaries. She didn't just give a message and go, but rather she stayed for a long time speaking with the visionaries like a friend or a mother. She would ask about their families and their surroundings and allow them to play with her, laugh and dance for her. Our Lady gave an answer to those who thought this way when she said, "*Blessed is the one who has somebody who spoils them, who cherishes them.*" She also said that she wants all children to behave like that in her presence. Our Lady desired that when we talk to her we should tell her all we have in our hearts, those things that worry us or make us happy, and that we should laugh with her when we are happy. She wants those private moments in prayer to be a time we can talk with her as though she was right there. She promises to love us and listen to us and spoil us. Here, *"spoil"* means loving her children kindly. Our Lady once said that she is not happy that people don't appreciate innocence anymore, they think of it as being stupid, but it is a sweet value.

She listened again for a while and then said:

"Thank you."

Then she said:

"Yes."

And then she started singing with a smile mixed with tears:

"I will tell everyone who will ask me about you, that the one who gave birth to Our Lord is incomparable. Be loved, be loved, be loved Mary. You, that Jesus chose to call His Mother, call me your child so I can trust. Be loved, be loved, be loved Mary etc...".

As she was singing, she seemed to lose her sight, her eye lashes began fluttering quickly, and all at once she fell down on her face on the bare cement and remained there without any noticeable injury or movement for about 15 minutes. When she began to regain her senses and strength, those around her picked her up and took her to her bedroom where she was able to rest for awhile. At 4:00 p.m., after she had regained her strength, they took her back out to the crowd where a multitude of people were waiting for her for hours, standing up, singing and dancing.

Alphonsine during an apparition, dancing for Our Lady.

At 4:00 p.m., November 28, 1989

Alphonsine immediately went to the podium where she had her public apparitions and waited there as all the people were joyfully singing songs of praise and worship to God the Father, Jesus, the Holy Spirit and to the Blessed Mother. While they were all singing and dancing, Alphonsine, in an instant, dropped to her knees like before. Looking up into the air her face seemed to show she was no longer part of this world, but of Heaven. As she gazed Heavenward, her arms began to raise up and spread open, in the same fashion as when we pray the Lord's prayer in Kibeho, and she started singing:

"We are greeting you Mother of God, Virgin Mary please pray for us, Virgin Mary please pray for us, Virgin Mary please pray for us. We are greeting you like Angel Gabriel a long time ago."

In reply to Our Lady, Alphonsine said:

"Not too much, I have been thinking about it as you told me earlier and as you told me the last time we met. All these months I have been trying to remind myself that this will be the very last time. The first two months I suffered a lot, but slowly I am getting used to it. I tell myself that I don't have a choice, it has to be like that."

When Our Lady prepares the visionaries for her farewell, she reminds them that she loves them as much as she loves each one of us and that she was there for a reason.

She had been sent by God to deliver a message. She knew how painful it would be for the children not to see her anymore, and she helped them to understand so they could bear it, but she also told them that while we are still on earth, suffering is a part of our daily bread. She taught them how to accept and suffer well and that suffering leads to heaven. Suffering teaches us many things we would not otherwise learn. Each person carries a cross, but what is important is to offer our sufferings to God and live through them without complaining. On earth we are still in exile, but once we are in heaven we will be happy as we will have reached our ultimate destination of joy.

She then said:

"*Yes.*"

And then added:

"*I feel strong in my heart somehow, given the way I prepared myself, I feel that strength in my heart and I am thankful.*"

She smiled and continued listening silently, and after a short time she said:

"*I have been thinking about it, and I look at how big I am! When you first came to visit me I was a small child, I don't mean such a small child, but I was a child in many ways. Look at me now, I am a big girl. I would even say that you raised me, since I was a teenager until now. I am very thankful. You gave me all the tools I need to be on my own. I am not a child anymore and I promise you to do good, because I know you will never be far from me.*"

When Alphonsine talks about the tools to be on her own, I remember in a special way when I came to understand the value of the prayer of the rosary and how powerful it is. Also, the power of the celebration of the Eucharist, novena, fasting, the reading and meditation on the Bible, etc... all those spiritual tools we have been given. For example, Our Lady said that we should pray the rosary for world peace and for our own. In Rwanda, Our Lady told us that if we had said the rosary in our villages, the horrific genocide would not have happened. This warning was given to us 12 years before the genocide and we didn't listen. To know the value of that prayer is a gift I will always cherish. The rosary is a summary of the life of Christ in the Bible. It is a very powerful prayer since we join with Mary in meditating on the life of Christ in its entirety in one prayer. Our Lady told us that through the rosary prayed from the heart, we can obtain an answer to our prayers and even wars can be stopped. You see, anyone who prays the rosary is capable of receiving many graces, so there is no reason to lose hope or to despair in life because Jesus told us, *"Ask and it shall be given, knock it shall be opened..."* It is up to us to know how to ask through prayer and fasting and I promise you, if God doesn't give you what you want, He will give you better, and if He doesn't give you what you are praying for at all, He will reveal to you why what you were asking was not good for you. He is the most loving Father. I will never forgot when my father told us that he prayed the rosary for two years for me to get a scholarship in a school of his choice. Two years later when I passed the exam they randomly placed me in the school he prayed for. It was very hard to get a scholarship as a teenager so this was a great grace. That moment changed everything in the way I viewed life, all things are possible if we can be faithful in prayer. Since the time I lost my parents in the genocide there have been many moments of loneliness. However, whenever I feel this I pray the rosary and my peace always returns. When I need a friend, when I need a job, when my children and I are sick, when I go through trouble of any kind, again, I pray the rosary over and over and God never fails to answer, in His time, but He is never too late for you. Our Lady also guided and reminded us of the power and value of love and kindness and the value of self sacrificing for love. It was the greatest commandment Our Lord left us, "*Love one another as I have loved you, and love God above all*". You can never go wrong by loving truly but, sooner or later, you will always go wrong by hurting or hating others; and if you realize you have gone wrong, Jesus forgives you always, every present moment is a new beginning.

She then listened for a while and then responded:

"*So many times you spoke about the Rosary, the prayer you love so much, the importance of going to confession, and you also told me that you love Christians who obey the Church and the leaders of the Church. You told me that you want people to love you and to encourage others to love you. Other personal messages you gave me, I gave them to those they were meant for. I am grateful to you because I saw that many messages were well received and put into practice. This is the last time I am seeing you like this, I mean I don't want to call it the very last, because I will always remember you. I am very grateful that you chose me, and you trusted me even though I know you always told me that you would help me. I really felt your help in everything, you keep your promises. There is nothing I can remember where you didn't intervene when I needed you in all these years we were together. Now that you are saying goodbye to me, I will be comforted to know that you said that you will always be with me even when I can't see you to talk to you like this. Everything was well received by all the people you sent me to, even those who gave me a hard time at first; in the end it was all good, all honor is yours, and I thank you because those people kept your words and none forgot your message to them. So these days I was on retreat, I reflected on all that. Some other people you sent me to, I finally met them. They are those I met here at school that were happy just to be present on this holy ground of Kibeho and it gave them so much joy. Sometimes, foreigners wrote me letters telling me how being here changed their lives and made them so happy. I really thank you when I see even those who didn't understand our language saying that they have been touched and got a lot from being here, it is so wonderful! All those I spoke to wanted you to come back to visit, at least once more, but I told them that we must get used to it, it will never be the right time for you to say goodbye to us. I am glad that you too are happy with the fruits of your visit."*

Many people have asked why Our Lady was happy with the fruits that were born in Rwanda from her visit, even though the genocide happened? To this, I think that we should always remember that Our Lady's main goal was not only to prevent the genocide, but to prepare hearts to love God and earn heaven. The prediction of the genocide was not the only message either. The main message was that we should learn to love one another and if everyone did not listen to Our Lady, it doesn't mean that many didn't listen and grow in love towards their neighbor. I remember Our Lady saying that if her warning came to pass, not to cry for those who would die because the gates of heaven would be open for them as they will have died innocently. She said, *"Cry for those who will remain alive because many will be tempted to violence and revenge. Others will not be able to bear to live with the wrong they have done to others."* She said, *"There will be some who will be left, they will be left to tell of the goodness of God, because there is nothing else that could console them after the pain they would have experienced."* Only God could give the grace of peace for this was beyond their own ability. I believe the grace of God was with Rwanda because our good and wise God used the bad to bring a greater good. I don't have any doubt that the prosperity of Rwanda today, the light it gives to the world and the example of reconciliation it is to the world, is a result of the mercy of God. This country could have sunk forever, never to be heard from again, but instead, the recovery of Rwanda amazes the world. It is those fruits Our Lady is talking about, which have led to our country recovering so quickly. Our Lady said that the world will one day come to kneel on this holy ground, in Kibeho, in this tiny country where Our God has chosen to send His Mother to give a message for the world.

It was also very nice for me to hear that there is nothing Alphonsine remembers happening where Our Lady didn't intervene when she needed her. She is talking here about those moments in life when she was not seeing Our Lady or able to ask her for help in person. It is during these times and in times of difficulty that Alphonsine turned to prayer. As Our Lady hears and answers her, she will also listen and answer us when we decide to call upon her intercession. One day we will look back and realize that she really did answer all our prayers. Our Lady reminded the children many times that she loves us all and intercedes for each one of us the same. She will come to our help and never leave us alone with our troubles. We have a comforter and a Father who is rich beyond our imagining and who loves us beyond our comprehension.

She listened intently for a while and then said:

"I think about everything and I think it was necessary, even if I suffered a lot on the way. You know how people are. We are proud, we don't like to get our feelings hurt, but I think it was necessary for me to go through it. All I had to suffer, I now understand that

it was necessary for me to go through it to know the truth, and learn more about life. You see, if one lives without problems, one will never learn the lessons that one learns through resolving those problems. It wouldn't be good to live without problems."

What Alphonsine says is a result of what Our Lady has been teaching her for nine years and we should take it seriously as well. I think if it was not the truth or for us as well, Our Lady could have made it so we didn't hear it, or she would have corrected her in a way we understood. Many people ask themselves what is the best way to deal with pain and difficulties in their lives. They ask why bad things happen to good people? To hear Alphonsine talking about the good in our suffering is a gift from heaven. We need to learn from her response, and it is true, if you have never been tested by an occasion that teaches you how to be patient, how can you say that you are a patient person? Good people also learn from bad experiences and that strengthens them even more. Only God reads our hearts, we all need Him. There are so many lessons in life we can only learn and discover by going through them and dealing with them personally. I knew one person who was very successful in his work and had a phone company. I asked him how he started and he told me, it was through mistakes he made that he learned how to avoid them in the future and that made him very successful. I pray daily that I have the strength to bear the crosses in my life, that I am capable to bear pain, without ignoring the lessons hidden in them. No one loves pain and suffering, but it is like being a student who wants to graduate with honors, but doesn't want to miss a party due to studying, writing papers or doing home work; but we learn those things are necessary for the greater joy of academic achievement. To reach our destination we must endure pain and make sacrifices.

Listening some more she then said:

"You have told me that you would be back. You told me the last day you would come so that people will know in advance and be happy. They won't say that you didn't give them enough time to prepare."

More than anything, Our Lady is talking about emotional preparation so that people will not feel disappointed, as they would be if she were to say goodbye suddenly. When Our Lady comes to visit, she visits everyone. That is how we felt when she was speaking to the visionaries. In preparation for Our Lady's visit people bought new clothes and prepared themselves. In response, Our Lady always acknowledged those who were there. She was so happy the people came and her love for everyone was so great! She gave us advice on how to live in this life. These were truly precious and cherished moments with Our Lady! This heavenly visit was sad for everyone and everyone felt the heart-wrenching pain when Our Lady said goodbye. Our Lady was concerned about people being accepting and prepared for her farewell, which was also a loving act on her behalf. Our Lady has such a loving motherly heart that she helped prepare Alphonsine and everyone for this moment a year earlier. People begged for her to stay longer, but as she gave Alphonsine the grace to bear the separation, we felt as if we had received it as well. Although she is no longer present to us through the visionaries, her presence is still felt to this day in Kibeho. I can recall one day when I was about to leave Rwanda and had been pregnant for six months. I felt like I had to go to say goodbye to Our Lady, but in the meantime my doctor had told me that I should not travel long distances in the car. However, I thought about it and I knew in my heart that Our Lady who is the Mother of God would never let my child be hurt if I was going to her, so I went to Kibeho to pray on the grounds. Later, my first child was born two weeks late, very strong and healthy. Our Lady always made us feel that the things we do out of love for her will never go unnoticed, and that she will fix what is not fixed, especially if we are sincere in our good intentions. We have a powerful Mother who is accessible all the time. We would be cheating ourselves not to get to know her and enjoy that incredible love of our spiritual Mother. Can you imagine a child who doesn't know their mother when they are both alive? If so, the best thing you could do for that child would be to arrange for the child to meet the mother. This would mean the world to this child. For those people you encounter that don't know Our Lady, you are encouraged to introduce them to their heavenly Mother. For those who do know her, remind them of what a loving Mother they have. Hardly ever will you be sad again if you are close to her.

Alphonsine listened and then said:

"Ooh that is very nice. I am happy you are happy for everyone. It is understandable that there are those who can't be here because they don't have money to travel this far, or they are not aware of today's apparitions, but the most important thing is that you look in their hearts and you know their intentions. And those from foreign countries, it is possible that they remembered the day you appeared to me first and they might have heard that it is the same date you are saying goodbye to me and maybe they remembered to celebrate with us in their home countries, if they didn't have the means to be here today. All that is possible as you just told me. The most important thing is that what they heard when they were here will continue to live and grow in their hearts."

This answer also reveals that Our Lady first gave those words of understanding to those who couldn't make it to Kibeho due to various reasons. This reminds me that God judges our intentions more than our ignorance for He knows our hearts. This encourages me to always try to appeal to God who sees our heart and who is loving and merciful. We should never be ashamed of our sins. Rather in all humility, we should show Him our hearts for He sees them anyway. It is truly better to be open and honest with God rather than trying to hide from Him, who sees all. When you come to realize that, you will tolerate others much easier because you will also understand how our God who sees all tolerates you. Why does He even keep us alive if we hurt Him so much? Because He has hope for us. We all have the capacity to change as long as we live, and we should pray for each other to find that grace to change rather than hating each other for the wrong we do.

She listened and said:

"I did as you told me to do and as is expected of every good Christian. Normally, all Christians should listen to the Church, as you spoke about that many times. I have been praying for them also, entrusting all to you. To this day, they are not discouraged, I saw some of them at school, and it must be a special grace they received to keep them going. Besides, they have other responsibilities, a lot, it is not easy. You know what they need most and how to help them, make it easy for them, so that the outcome of their work will be useful to the rest of the world."

I couldn't tell what Alphonsine was referring to exactly, but I am guessing this refers to those commissioned to investigate the apparitions. Some of them were doctors who were still working full time jobs, while others were theologians who were priests and active in their parishes. Alphonsine fully cooperated and supported this work they were doing. She prayed that God would grant them discernment and good judgment, and that He would grant them the necessary time needed to accomplish this important work that concerned the world.

Listening again, she responded by saying:

"I thank you so much for that as well, you gave me strength to accomplish that, because I didn't feel impatient to listen to their questions. I actually felt happy to answer them. I didn't complain about things they did, they had to do. I am thankful for the patience I felt because, as people, we tend to be proud. On my own, I could not have accepted being in that situation. It was not by my strength that I let people do to me what they wanted so they could be sure of what they wanted to know. Thank you for giving me the humility and the obedience to do what I am asked to do regardless."

I am guessing she is talking about the members of the commission again. It was said that the doctors performed many medical tests on the visionaries, which were very uncomfortable. They were put to sleep, given medications to see their mental responses, had all kinds of machines connected to their bodies to see what their mental state was or if there was any other mental abnormality. They said they had to test them to determine if they were lying. One psychiatric doctor told me that during the apparition, he had to perform some tests that could have easily killed them. He did things like holding their throats down that normally would cut off their ability to breathe. They were hit in places which under normal circumstances would cause a loss of consciousness. Their skin was burned and needles were stuck into them while they were having the apparitions. It is amazing that they never reacted to any of them, and yet when they tried any of these tests while in a normal state, they reacted like everyone else would. This doctor told me that the bishop at the time was very mad at him when he saw the extent of tests he was performing on the children.

I love the fact that Alphonsine includes herself as one of the people who are proud when she said, "We people, we tend to be proud." I think we all carry that human weakness in us and those sins with us. Some may have simplicity or humility, but not enough of it. Some have not killed, but maybe in thought have wished someone was dead. Some may not have physically committed adultery but maybe in their mind they did. The lesson in all this to me is that what we reproach others for, we are really guilty of ourselves in many ways. We should always remember to pray for ourselves when we feel like reproaching others and judging others in their actions or words, or when we are talking about the mistakes of others. We should try to treat others, without knowing whether they are guilty or not, with the same compassion we would like to be treated with if we were the ones found guilty.

She listened again and said:

"You also told me that you would not come to visit me in private as much and that I shouldn't rely on it much. I understand I will be like every other Christian. I will try to follow the example you gave me, all the lessons you taught me. I will try to put them into practice, so that I can accomplish the mission you gave me. I think that you gave me many examples. Now if I see somebody doing wrong, I will not wait for you to come and tell me to go tell them to correct themselves for their sake, I will tell them myself.

So now I understand that I have tools and I have been given the means and strength to do what I have to do and I have trust in you that you will continue to help me. I will have to do things for others without having to say that you told me to do so. Please help me always, Mother, to accomplish that for it is not easy. There are those people who have a lot of faith so that, when they hear that it is you who said to do a thing, they would do it at all cost for you, because they know it came from you. So if I tell them on my own to do something, they might say that I am not having apparitions anymore and what I am telling them is my own judgment and they might not listen to me. I beg you to give me strength to not get discouraged because I also know that apostles don't live in total peace, especially when they want to say the truth or correct somebody. I also want to ask you in this moment to please give me strength to carry on what you want of me in my future and in my life now, with happiness".

I especially love the fact that Alphonsine takes this responsibility to live in truth and to help others do the same. Sadly the world we live in today is not open to someone saying they are not doing right. They will tell you not to invade their lives and who are you to know what is right and wrong? On the other hand, people have used lies to manipulate others and so it becomes confusing to many when someone really has their best interest at heart. There is so little love among people that we tend to not know what the real motivation is. However, this is an important action of love to practice. We should love people enough to show them where they might be going wrong, but we must approach correcting others with a lot of prayer and kindness. We have to be able to find the right moment and be ready to explain why what we are telling them they are doing wrong, is truly wrong. It is important to show the person the consequences of their wrongdoing. My father was very much loved, but he wasn't one you got along with if you were misbehaving. I remember he used to spank us when we did wrong, but he never spanked us out of anger. When he found out about how we had misbehaved he would set up an appointment with you to punish you at night after work and teach you a lesson. Our neighbors would even bring their children for him to punish them. I remember one time when my friends and I ran after a car that was driving away from my village and he called us together that night and told us that he was going to spank us for running after the car and do it in front of the other parents as well. He explained to us that if the car had stopped suddenly it could have hurt us, caused an accident or even killed someone. He told us how sad people would feel if people no longer came to visit our village anymore out of concern that children there run after your car like they want to try and steal something from you. He said it is not polite and it will drive guests away from the village. He reminded us that good children have to behave and act with prudence. We all asked for forgiveness from our parents and as a punishment my dad made us lie down and gave us a stick across our behinds four times. We cried, but no one felt bad in our hearts that it was unfair after realizing all the damages we could have caused our parents and neighbors. We didn't mean that, but we realized we didn't think about it either. Good friends beckon each other back in the right direction, but especially among adults, it must be done with respect. It is best to ask the person if they thought about the consequences. We are all prophets to one another, and even if it might not seem peaceful in the first place, we must hold to the truth and defend truth. By doing this we will always have peace in our hearts since it was done for the sake of truth and righteousness. I think that the worse sin of our generation is the deliberate confusion we bring to the truth. It is true that we all sin and fall into wrongdoing, but it is a grave sin to defend the wrong, and want to make it right because we don't want to feel like we have done wrong. God will always forgive us, but how can He forgive us if we don't even recognize what is wrong? It is important to keep that clear, it is important to read the Bible and keep the truth clear to us.

She listened and said:

"You know us people, we are like that, we are hard-hearted. When we want to do something, we do it, but when we make our hearts so hard, we become hard. But I am happy to know that you who look into the hearts of people can see that there are many people who have understood your message. It gives me great joy to know that your visit and our efforts were not in vain and that you are happy with our efforts."

The good news is that although we are hard-hearted, it is good to recognize that Our Lady still chose to come to Alphonsine even though she included herself among the hard-hearted like the rest of us. As Our Lady told us, pray for everything, even our own weaknesses. It is really as simple as that. It is good for us to wake up in the morning and ask God, *"Soften my heart dear Lord, that I may always do your most holy will, and that I have the wisdom to know right from wrong. Help me not to be an obstacle to those blessings you wish to grant me or others."* You will be amazed that by just saying a prayer like this, it will begin to change things around. You will surprise yourself in how you react differently when you thought you were going to be stubborn. Stubborn people know in their hearts that acting in this way works against them, but the temptation seems so strong that they succumb to the temptation and act in a stubborn manner despite the consequences that might follow. The greatest gift Our Lady has given us is the capacity and the reminder to pray, to pray unceasingly. It is through prayer that we are born again daily and find the strength to amend our lives. Pray as you wake up and pray before you go to sleep, but even throughout the day, pray short ardent prayers, *"Jesus I love you, I trust in you, take my heart... my Lady I love you... God you are almighty, I am all yours..."* They will make a difference in the peace you feel within your heart.

Grace works in miraculous ways and we just have to trust its effects when we do our best. I remember one time I was going to meet a friend of mine. I had promised to send him a letter, but somehow it slipped my mind and I forgot to send it to him. A few weeks later when I was going to meet him I was ill at ease about how I would be able to face him, what would I tell him? If I told him the truth, he would think poorly of me, that I don't keep my promises. In my own mind it didn't seem too bad, but my heart was aching to face that embarrassment. My fear was that he may not even believe me. So I had a big temptation come into my heart in which I would send a letter out that day and lie to him that I sent it early, but my heart was not at ease with this and it bothered me to have to lie. I started to feel resentment towards him, like he was the one pushing me to lie. I was trying to convince myself that if he was a kinder person I would feel comfortable telling the truth, but this was really my issue not his since he didn't even know what was going on. So one part of me was telling me to lie and avoid the pain of the embarrassment, another part of my heart was saying that it is okay to tell the full truth and take that pain and leave it up to the person to trust me or not. I had such an enormous fear, which was almost controlling my actions. In the end, I remembered when Our Lady told us that we should pray for anything, even if it is to pray for sincerity or the strength to say the truth. So I asked Our Lady to give me the strength to accept my mistake and admit to the full truth even if it should cause me to faint. Later when I met the person, he never asked me about the letter and I ended up confessing to him of my laziness and forgetfulness. He only smiled and told me that he didn't think it was such a priority. I had so much peace in my heart telling him and never felt the slightest embarrassment. That really reminded me of the power of God's grace, how it works, and that we can't predict how things will turn out. It reminded me that I should always hold on to the truth no matter what, and God will take care of the rest. His yoke is easy, however, it is the crosses that we bring upon ourselves through own weaknesses that are heavier.

After listening she then said:

"Yes, for those things that didn't go as well as you wanted them to go, you know them. It is understandable that everything would not have gone so perfectly, we will continue to pray, to pray a lot so that all the messages will bear good fruits and so that everything will go well. There are those who get it now and those who will understand later, and some who will get it after those alive today have all died. The most important thing is that your name and your words in Kibeho will never be forgotten. Thank you."

It is so important that we are trying to live in the truth, to remember that we don't live just for ourselves, but that we are also paving the way for our children and the generations to come. We should never be discouraged if things are not working out our way. In each moment of our lives we should only do what we believe is good in the eyes of God. If He doesn't use our good efforts and works now, He may use them at a later time. When we teach our children a way to live, we are showing our care and concern for what tomorrow holds for them and their children. We must hold on to truth and the right values as they will bear fruits sooner or later.

She listened and then started to sing:

"I will reach among the people of all nations. I will tell everyone without forgetting anyone. I will tell them the message you gave me. I will give your message, Beautiful Mary, Our Mother. Mother of the Word, I am here before you. Give me the message you want me to take, I will deliver it, I will deliver it, I will deliver it."

Many times Our Lady requested songs from the visionaries and many times Our Lady would teach us a message through the songs which she desired to give to the people. Sometimes Our Lady even taught songs to the children, a melody that was never heard before. She said that singing Godly songs is praying twice. On other occasions, she asked children to sing and dance to songs we already knew from church. I am sure it was a great compliment and honor for those who wrote those songs to have Our Lady choose them. The songs were all beautiful and sang praises to God. Everyone was able to sing along because they were songs we all knew and had sung many times. She also chose those songs which were easy to dance to so we all danced in the joy of the Lord. The funny part was that the visionary didn't know we were there, so she sang at her own rhythm and sometimes it would take everyone a little bit of time to adjust and at other times we found ourselves singing behind or ahead of her. Many times Our Lady would ask the visionary to repeat a part of the song and we would all be singing the next part already. We would all then stop and follow the lead of the visionary as we knew Our Lady was the one orchestrating everything. My memories are filled with the joy we all had that day and the many signs Our Lady obtained for us to show us the authenticity of her presence.

She listened and said many times:

"Yes, yes, yes..."

And then said:

"I understand that you wanted to correct us, sometimes a child changes their ways when they perceive the sadness of a parent. So if your sadness and tears sometimes made many remember to change their ways, I am happy for that."

> I was so happy to hear that Our Lady even valued the reaction of the people to her tears. When a mother is trying to bring children to the truth, she will do anything. In my culture it is a big deal for a mother to cry. Generally, it is perceived that if the mother is crying it is because all the children must have failed. In Rwanda, as a child you want to grow up and make your parents proud of having you, and if a mother has to cry, it means you failed in some way, not only to make her proud, but you even caused her pain. When a child saw that he was causing his mother pain it would result in the child reviewing and trying to correct his behavior. Well, for the many who didn't change when Our Lady cried it can mostly be attributed to the fact that they didn't believe she was appearing and they never made the connection that she was their mother. But for those who believed in the apparition and who knew in the smallest way that she was their mother, they did their best to amend their ways.

Alphonsine listened for a while and then she spoke as though she was conveying a message that was to be given to those present. She said:

"My children, saying goodbye to you doesn't mean that I am forgetting Africa, not even the whole world. It doesn't mean that I am going to forget Rwandans. Alphonsine was my instrument, she is not your God. I am asking you not to forget the love I have loved you with, when I came to your country. I am asking you not to forget the trips you have made to Rwanda."

> In these words, Our Lady reminded me that it is not enough for her to have come and visited us, nor is it enough for her to say that she loves us, but what is most important is to accept the love she offers to us. If you are given a gift and you never open it, what is that gift worth? Nothing! It can be the best gift ever, but it is worthless if it is not accepted with love. Many people will ask themselves, so what do you want me to do about all this you have shared with us? Thank Our Lady for loving you and think about or read about the messages of Kibeho often as we must be reminded of the message continually. Ask Our Lady to touch your heart and make it sensitive to her love, and ask that you may love her and God more. As I think back during the genocide, I realize I was able to feel the love of God in such a tangible way, and it left me thirsting for more. Since then, I often remember to ask God, "Show me more of your love and help me to love you more."

She again listened and then said many times:

"Yes... yes... yes ..."

And then she said:

"You know it has to be like that. I have accepted the situation, and I am happy. I am not sad anymore and I try not to get upset anymore because something happens by surprise or doesn't work out

how I planned it. I see those things as God's will, and I try to do good things for Him."

For those who have read my book *Left To Tell*, you may remember how I was so mad at my parents when they asked me to leave school to come and spend the Easter holiday with them in 1994. I had an exam after the following week, and most of my school mates stayed at school to study together. I too had asked my parents if I could stay at school like everyone else in my class, and they said no. I decided to go home, not because I thought it made sense, but out of obedience to my parents. I was mad, but I didn't show it to them. I tried to explain my reasons for wanting to stay at school, but my father said no and that was it. However, little did I realize that three days into my vacation the genocide was going to start, and everyone who stayed at school that week would be attacked and murdered. The killers sent by the government waited until the students went to the school restaurant where they all met at the same time in the evening and they burned the two restaurants with bombs and grenades killing everyone there. I am not saying that I was fortunate not to be among them, but we all have a path and a purpose in life. Today, I can't say I wish I had stayed at school. Would this have been the right thing to do? Was it better for me to obey my parents who missed me and wanted this vacation together as a family or should I have stayed at school? That week became my last vacation with them. When I think about it today, I just wish I knew what God's will was. In the little wisdom I have gained through that experience, we will never know definitively everything God wants, but one thing I am sure of is that we should always make decisions based on love. Don't leave somebody home who is sick without arranging help for them because you have to go to work or dinner. Don't pass somebody by in an accident because you have a meeting that can't be postponed. We should always follow the voice of love and kindness in our hearts sincerely, not making excuses. God will guide you to what is meant to be. Don't cause your heart to be troubled by complaining about all that is going on in your day, rather, be alert and do your best. As Alphonsine said, she doesn't let herself get upset now since she tries to accept all things as God's will. We should try to do the same in our daily lives.

She listened for a long while and then said:

"It is good that you will continue to help them. I know you will never forget those you have loved so much by coming to visit them from heaven. That alone will encourage them knowing that you will always be at their side."

She then said after listening:

"Let's hope in that. It is true, you could not have come in vain. When you won't be here anymore, we will be comforted in remembering that you left happy with our efforts and that will give us the strength to do our best to follow your message and live our lives as people who have had a chance to know you. With your help and the help of God, we will accomplish what you want of us so we can make you happy always."

As a mother, I love the encouragement Our Lady gives us. Some things did not go as she wished, but in general she leaves happy with the outcome of her visit and she let us know that. Let us encourage one another by seeing the best in people, our friends, our families and not dwelling on what is negative.

She listened for a long while. During the conversation she

would at times answer by saying yes and then she responded:

"Since you know, please give them the strength they need. I have not seen them a lot at school except during the past three to four years. In that short time they were blessed to come to the ground where you chose to give a message for the world. When they go back to their homes, please help them to remember what they have heard, to live so that their efforts to come here will not have been in vain. Give them the grace to spread your messages, so they can bear many more fruits. And as for us Rwandans, as you just told us, we will not forget the love with which you have loved us by choosing our country to deliver a message to the whole world, and for choosing a simple place like Kibeho, a place I hear is unknown, but to me it seems to be very known."

I am thinking that maybe Our Lady was speaking about people from a certain country outside of Rwanda, possibly a group of people from a foreign country. We can see here Our Lady's concern, and Alphonsine's as well, that the message of Our Lady should bear fruit. This is what I hope for you who are reading this book, that you will try to live as the messages teach us, and spread them to those around you. Alphonsine talks about how people say that Kibeho is not known, when in her mind, it is very well known. It is funny that we grew up thinking that Rwanda was the whole universe, but when you get to know the world, it is then you realize that Rwanda itself as a country is unknown and very small. Kibeho itself is just a small village in Rwanda, which used to be the poorest of the villages in the whole country, however, with the apparition of Our Lady, it is changing. I love the innocence of Alphonsine, and as a Rwandan I understand her confusion about how a place that is visited by about thirty thousand people a year cannot be known in the world. It is when you

> put it in the perspective of other places that are known, like New York where I live now, and when I meet people everyday who think that Africa is one country, it is then that I know I come from an unknown place.

She smiled and then she kept listening looking tenderly to the one talking to her and then said:

"No, I am fine with it. I am happy and even if I wasn't happy, it is better when it is harder. All nine years are not for nothing."

> Here she reminds us that in the nine years that she has been speaking to Our Lady, she has become strong enough to carry her mission or whatever Our Lady is asking of her.

As she listened again, a smile appeared on her face and she said:

"You told me many times."

And then she listened again and started to sing:

"The child of Mary always has crosses she is bearing kindly. The child of Mary dies with many words in the heart. The child of Mary carries her cross with joy. The child of Mary sees the world as nothing."

She listened again and said:

"I remember that in the first days."

She continued to listen and she said, as if replying to somebody:

"You told me that the people in general are afraid of suffering. We love that nothing makes us suffer at all, but as you repeated to me many times, crosses teach us a lot as we become smarter, wiser. It

also gives each one of us an occasion to increase our love for God by showing Him that you can still do something for God, even when you are suffering like this."

She laughed and then said:

"I am happy that you know that. What makes us happy is that you have lived here and you have gone through all we go through, good and bad. But, I also hear that as years go by, the bad increases, but I am not sure how true that is. I am not sure if it is civilization that makes us forget about God. I hope that since you know and you see what we face, you will be helping us to accept things and deal with them. It is sad to see people who go to school and then accumulate a lot of intelligence, but then later go and write books to insult the Church, God and the people in the Church. For example, the Church or the country may give scholarships to people and then the top 6 out of 10 people who finish with the highest honors graduate, and they may leave and go write all they want, especially books where they may try to prove that God doesn't exist. Since you know about that as well, only God can give them light to understand the truth. Those kinds of people feel so above everyone else that they don't think they need anyone to show them the way since they think of themselves as smarter than everyone else. Give us the grace to respect God always. It is sad to see somebody growing up in the Church believing in God, and then they grow up, get rich and start to deny God. You see God lives with the humble, and when the material things get into their minds, they forget God and then they come to deny Him. I am glad that you know and see those kind of people. It is only you who can correct them. You have many ways to show them that their way is not right. Because for us, if we try to tell them to stop their ways, they think we don't know what we are talking about."

She listened and after a long while, she said:

"Yes…yes…"

And at times she would appear surprised by what she was hearing, and at other times, she would laugh or just smile. She then spoke as if trying to repeat something she was told:

"My children, pray, pray, follow the Bible and the Gospel of my Son so you will always have peace in your heart. My Son suffered so much, He was humiliated, He was persecuted, but He still is the King of Heaven and Earth."

She continued to repeat:

"You all who are called crazy because you like to pray, all of you who are called thieves, those to whom they say that you are losing time by giving your life to God, I tell you one day you will be happy."

She listened and she said:

"Yes."

And then started to sing:

"I will tell them that the one who will go into the Kingdom of Heaven is the one who has worked to go there, it is the only way. I will deliver your message."

After singing, she listened once again and then said:

"You told me, it has been a while, but I haven't been thinking about it that much. I don't know why. Oh, is that it? If that is the one, it is really an unusual flower, very special. If you try to pierce it, it wouldn't pierce. For anyone to have such a special thing, that

can separate them from others, and sometimes even suffer for it, and knowing they must do it because it is God's will, it is really a great thing, but not everyone is so brave."

This is one of those messages that you might not figure out exactly what Our Lady was saying to Alphonsine since the word used in Kinyarwanda that I translated as pierce, is called "Gutobora." It means to make a hole in something. She didn't use tear so I tried to translate it as it is. I remember there was a time Our Lady requested Anathalie to have a plastic flower in the chapel as a sign of a soul that is always alive and beautiful and never dies. In Rwanda, flowers grow everywhere all through the year, to a point where the Germans that colonized Rwanda called it the country of the eternal springtime. The weather is nearly perfect as it varies between 65 and 75 degrees throughout the year. It is never humid, not too cold and not too warm. However, plastic flowers are very rare in Rwanda. For Our Lady to use it to signify something spiritual is very meaningful to us Rwandans, because plastic flowers are loved and are rare. I can see that if this example was given in the USA where I live now, it wouldn't have much significance, not because people wouldn't accept what Our Lady is trying to say, but because plastic flowers are not seen as something rare and beautiful since they are not real. But, our wise and good Mother knows how to speak to us in the language we understand and work through things that are familiar to us. Truly everything depends on how we want to look at them, and what meaning we give them. And so it is with our intentions, since purity and sin lies in the intentions of the heart. But in this message, I wonder if anyone who was given that flower from heaven would be a cause for others to be jealous?

She listened again and then said:

"You have told me already. I thought it was the usual message, like others you gave me for my life that will be for the future."

She listened for a while and then said to those who were there as if repeating what Our Lady said:

"My children, I give you my blessing. I am not giving it only to those who are here in Kibeho, but also to those in the world."

She kept listening intently. Seeming a little worried she said:

"No, but there are times when somebody comes to visit you and you forget that they will leave, then when they say one little thing, that thing makes you feel like maybe they are about to leave."

> This is one way Our Lady prepares Alphonsine for the fact that she is about to leave so she can be strong emotionally and Alphonsine got it. She must have asked Our Lady if she is leaving, because normally Our Lady would give her a blessing at the end of the apparition, which are her last words. In hearing these words I can feel Alphonsine's heart jumping out of sadness thinking Our Lady is leaving. However, Our Lady out of love and respect for our culture stayed a little bit longer after giving the blessing she usually gives at the end.

She listened for a long while and then said as though repeating what she was told:

"All of you who are sick with incurable sicknesses, a good heart surpasses all, there are no riches that are beyond a clean heart. All of you who have had difficulties of all kinds, there are difficulties everywhere, in all walks of life. When they don't go away, offer them to God. Every good Christian is requested to

offer a sacrifice. All of you who have problems in your families, think of the Holy Family, who lived in such poverty, and who lived among those who didn't like them nor understand them, and with the problems you have, come close to them. All of you who have dedicated your lives to God, a life like that is not easy. The most important thing is to be faithful to your promises. All of you young people, when you are young, you think that you can do anything; be careful not to fall and damage yourself for good. All of you leaders, who have the capacity to represent many people, don't kill, but save. Don't be greedy, but share with others, and don't attempt to hurt those who are trying to expose your wrongdoings. I tell you, anyone you want to hurt because they love people and are defending human rights, because they are defending the cause of the poor and the simple, because they are defending anything good and trying to love God, I tell you, whatever you do will be in vain."

> For some of you reading this book, you may not be familiar with the Holy Family, it is the family of St. Joseph, Mary and Jesus during their time on earth. Today, they are still called the Holy Family and are an example to families. Many churches around the world are named after "The Holy Family".

She listened and then said:

"Yes, you are right."

Listening again she said:

"I have been watching, you see we try to see the wrong in people instead of trying to see what is good. When people do good, we try to hide it, when they do wrong, we publicize it. I hope you come to our help because you know our problems. Some of those really need your

intervention, as for us we can't do anything about it. Sometimes we can do something about the situation, other times, we just need you."

> Our Lady repeated to us in Kibeho many times, not to rush to see the bad in people and even if we do see it, to be charitable and pray for them or try to help them change in a kindly manner. She said, rather than talking to others about their wrongdoings or weaknesses, we must think of everyone like we think of those people we love the most. If it is your mother you love a lot, your dad, your child, your boyfriend, girlfriend, wife or husband or a good friend, before you say something about somebody, respond as if it was that person you love most that did it. If you would respond in the same way, if you truly think you would, then maybe you are doing right. If you think you would protect the one you love, have the courage to protect another person as well. It should and must be love that guides our actions and our decisions.

She listened again and then kept saying:

"Yes, yes, yes…"

And then said:

"No, I am not tired. I just think that when you are talking to a higher personality in general, you have to be humble. To be on my knees is what I found worthwhile right now as I always do."

She listened and then said:

"Thank you."

She then said:

"It is only you who can make a difference in that situation. I will continue to pray about it. Since you spoke about people of every

walk of life, as Christians we will be praying for everybody, we will be praying for children, our leaders, for families, and for those who dedicated their lives to God. To hear the messages is one thing, but to put them into practice is another thing. It is not easy."

From the time the apparition began she was kneeling on the ground. After she said thank you, she stood up while they kept conversing. When Our Lady says to pray for everybody, she really means everybody and many times we forget. There is one time I remember in Kibeho when two students who were Muslims were persecuted a lot after the apparitions. Everyone told them that the true religion is Catholicism since Our Lady is appearing here in Kibeho. They were the only two who were Muslims and others told them they would go to hell. Well, even those who were having the apparitions were persecuted as well for lying and those who didn't believe were also persecuted by others who believed. The next time Our Lady came to appear, she told the visionary to tell everyone to leave her children alone. She said, "You are all my children, regardless of which religion you practice. If any of you was born in a place where you were not told of Jesus, would you know Him? God will judge people from what they know and how they have exercised love in their hearts and the commandments of their religion." Many times, Our Lady told us to pray the rosary not as Catholics, but as her children. She speaks to us as her children, and her messages are not for Catholics alone because they know of her, but she speaks to all of us, even those who don't know her. We need to all listen to her and respond.

She said *"Yes"* to what was told to her and then started to sing:

"Mary, Mother of the Word, please come to our help so we

*can understand. Mary Mother of God, come to our help so we can
understand..."*

She kept listening and then said to those who were there:

**"My children, in truth, I am not staying as long as I used to
do as I have told you all that was necessary. I have just told you
what more I needed from you. As I said, I want to remind you
that I am happy. I am happy with the fruits that were born in
Rwanda since I came here. Don't worry about the difficulties
you have. Nothing is better than having God. My dear children,
problems exist everywhere, but the most important thing is to
have an accepting heart without complaining."**

> I can see in these words my mom speaking to me when
> she came to visit us. "Honey, I am not staying as long as I
> usually do...," to remind me she had come not because she
> had a lot of spare time, but because she had an important
> reason, maybe something she had to tell me or maybe
> because she missed me so much. Every word of Our
> Lady takes my breath away because it is said with such
> tenderness and each word reveals her motherhood. Here
> again, before she leaves she prepares Alphonsine a second
> time. She is about to leave but not quite yet. Like every
> caring mother who wishes to express their feelings of love
> so their child will feel secure, she desires that the child too
> should tell her whatever she wishes to say since she knows
> her mom is about to leave. At this point, I always feel a
> knot in my throat, like she is leaving me as well.

Alphonsine kept listening and then said:

*"Yes, I know now that I am not going to see you like this again.
I am grown up, this is it, I have to accept it. Actually I accepted it
the day you told me for the first time. But I am asking you, Mother,*

to give me strength to accomplish all you need of me, until my death. I am begging you to help me to be a good model everywhere I go or live, so that I won't be a reason for anyone to fall. I am asking you for help to save souls. I am asking you to help me to be a reason for joy in a good way, for those I will meet in my life. Please give me the grace to receive with kindness all those who will be coming to me, especially those who would like to know you through me. Grant that I may never complain about my work. Give me strength not to be tired and if I am, grant me patience. Give me the wisdom to know when I need to rest and rest only when I need to. I can see that my life is changing, my life has changed already. I used to live at school and I don't know what is awaiting me in life outside of school or how people live among themselves. I always followed the schedule in school and did what they told us to do every hour. Now I have to give myself a schedule and know what I have to do myself. But maybe since others have done it, I hope to be able to do it as well. However, some have made big mistakes when they misused the freedom outside school and have hurt themselves. This is why I am asking you to please be at my side. I fully trust in you. I will not ask you to do all for me, the strength you told me you gave me will carry me through, but please be with me. Allow me to love those who are of God that you will be sending me. Give me grace to love the poor, those who have nobody, and those who don't have anyone to understand them. Give me true kindness, the grace to live good with others. Give me humility, so that those who will come to me will find a welcoming soul so they don't get scared if it depends on how I behave towards them. Give me the grace to love prayer always. Give me the grace to teach others how to pray. Grant me the grace to forgive because I wouldn't live with anyone if I couldn't forgive, as we all make mistakes. Give me the grace to share the good I have. Don't let me be overfed when there is a hungry person at my door.

Give me the grace so I won't close the door to the hungry. Please help me not to tell anyone that I don't have time especially when what they need of me is important to their soul. In a few words, please help me to live like a good Christian, as God wants me to. All the years I will live outside of school, and the years I will live in the life you have revealed, please help me to live kindly with everyone. Help me to be happy just being called simple Alphonsine Mumureke, a person like any other, not necessarily the visionary. I don't mean to deny that I have seen you, unless people want to deny your visits, but help me to be happy to be seen like everyone else, to be known as me, not as anything special. Please help me so that wherever I will go people won't think of me as God or Mary, that they will see me as your instrument who was here only to deliver your message. Help them to remember that even someone who sees something in me will recognize that they too can be your messengers in their own ways, that every good Christian can be God's messenger. Help me to be treated like everyone else for I know that whenever I go by people they may refer to me as the one who had an apparition, and point fingers at me. That is okay, but Mother help me, so when I make friends or acquaintances and we are talking, they will not hold themselves back, but be free to be themselves or tell me whatever they want because they might remember that they are talking to the one who has seen you. I ask for your help so that people will not love me only during the time of their need of prayer. As I myself have lived that before, please, if possible, go into their hearts and change them from within. I can pray, but only you can change their hearts so that they will see me as a normal person. Mother, you know you gave me messages for myself and for other people, but I don't have the capacity to see into the future even though people sometimes think that I do. I am asking you Mother, and I know it is hard, but I am begging, even if I promise that I will not dislike anyone, sometimes it is so difficult. I am begging for help, that people who will see me will not love me too much just because I have had apparitions. There are many reasons people like each other. Sometimes we like one another because of the mercy we show to each other. Sometimes it is because another person has been kind to us, or because we had a wonderful conversation with them, even if we were not talking about God alone. These things make people like each other and become friends. Sometimes I too meet people in a bus, anywhere, and I like people because of what we talked about. Sometimes somebody who is polite makes you like them. You see, I wish for this kind of love and these types of natural interactions as ways of making friends, not people who show excessive love because of me being a visionary. I am asking you, but it doesn't have to happen how I want it all the time. I will accept whatever happens to me, but at least you know my wish. It will be difficult, but please give me the grace to know those kind of people so I recognize them."

The saddest and sweetest thing for me is that although Alphonsine was telling Our Lady that she is okay if she leaves and how prepared she is, she was still in tears most of the time. This reveals to me the acceptance I should have of God's will. Yes, our heart can be strong when the flesh is weak, but in those situations, even if there is pain, there is always peace. It is all about love, not anger or frustration, when we understand and say yes to those situations we don't want to accept, but to accept because it is God's will and He knows what is best. Somebody said that tears are close to love. Alphonsine's prayer to Our Lady should teach us how to talk to Our Lady and how to talk to Our Dear Father God and what to pray for. I would advise anyone to take up this prayer and make it yours and see if you even think of praying for those things that seem so important to us. Pride has become a way of living, and prayers like this help shape us in the way we are to do things. It is very useful for me and I hope it is for you as well.

She listened for a short while and then said:

"Thank you very much, that is so right. Yes, sometimes it helps some people to know who I am, that I have seen the Virgin Mary. Yes, it helps them. But you see for example, sometimes you make a friend and as I told you before they come to pray with you, and they all start saying let's go pray with her for she will get all the answers. I understand they can still get an answer, because after all it is God who answers prayers if we believe in Him. What I don't like are the times they receive the answer and then leave and never come back. You realize immediately the friend you thought you had wasn't real. For me it is good when we can pray for something together as friends and when the prayer is answered, the friendship remains. You see it hasn't happened that much, but I have seen it increasing. I understand we have to help people just for prayer, but if it is being confused with being friends and then leaving, please help us, and help them not to see me as their God. Don't let anyone see a letter from me and then think there are special blessings in my writings, because it is only me."

She listened, said:

"Yes."

And then said:

"Also, I offer you all the people in the world, but you told me that you already blessed each one of them, so I am asking you for another blessing on their behalf. I offer all those people who have helped me to make this message reach those it was meant for. They

had to be very patient many times when they were insulted just because they knew me, some for having been seen with me and others because they had helped me deliver the messages. Up to this day that you are saying goodbye to me, some of those people are really helping me and have been there for me. Those people treat me like a fellow Christian. They are praying for me, so please keep them and give them the necessary help they need. I am offering you those people, because what they did was for the love with which they love you and they thought that the way to help would be to help me to deliver your message, which you gave me. They were persecuted sometimes, insulted by others who believed that they did not know what they were doing. They were considered crazy, not smart, all kinds of bad stuff. I know you told me to pray for them, but I offer a special prayer for them as it is all I can do for them. I am not only praying for them alone, but that you give them special attention. Please give them extra strength. It is not easy for an elderly person, respectful and with integrity, to come to Kibeho and be the brunt of insults by others. It demands courage and a heart dedicated to God for a person to come to prayer places and receive insults and then still continue to go there and still feel joy. Please help Christians of the world to pray for those who have seen you, because many think that if we have seen you, our prayers are enough and we don't need anyone else's prayers. It is not true; we also need the prayers of our brothers and sisters. Please help them to think of us in their prayers so that we may all pray for one another. On earth, we don't have any other god than God the Father in Heaven. There is no other mother of mankind we have than you, Virgin Mary who lives in Heaven, who guides us daily.

My dear Mother, I think that is all I have to ask of you today. I already told you a lot on Saturday and Sunday morning. I hope I am not asking too much and I hope I haven't forgotten anything as I had so much to tell you, but what I told you summarizes all I had in my heart to ask you."

The Saturday and Sunday morning apparitions must have been the private ones with Our Lady. Alphonsine had prayed a great deal for all she had in mind. This is such a good lesson on how we should pray, and what not to forget. She prayed for everything and for everybody in the world, but also for her soul, her weaknesses, for all the confusion caused around her as a visionary. Sometimes we too are burdened and yet we forget to tell Our Lady about it. Even if you are confused and don't know how to pray and what to pray for, tell Our Lady that you are confused, as long as you have an ache somewhere in your heart, Our Lady cares and wants to hear about it, and so does Our God. One time Our Lady said that people pray without sincerity of heart and she said, "Pray for sincerity then and we will give it to you." We are so spoiled and so blessed. If only we knew how much we have been given and how to be happy for the graces we have been given rather than complaining about those things that are not going our way, our heaven would start here on earth. Our Lady used to teach us to pray this way, to talk to God and tell Him everything like a friend we trust so much. Imagine if you would meet such a friend, wouldn't you at least start by apologizing if there was something that didn't go well between the two of you? And then as good friends you would give each other a hug and forgive one another and begin to talk as true friends. Well this friend is not God, but Our Lady who wants to teach us the freedom we should have in front of Our God. After apologizing to God for our sins, we should thank Him for all the blessings He gives us daily and for all those He has given to us in our lives. Thank Him for life itself, look back and you will see so many blessings He has given you in your life. Then tell Him your troubles with deep trust because He loves you and He has the power to change them around. Tell Him those deep pains and wounds you carry within your heart, that place that no one else knows. He knows all things and He will never tell anyone and He will not even judge you. Our Lady promised, consolation will always come in one way or another. If you don't get better, you will understand why you are going through that. Remember that nothing lasts forever, only God.

She listened again and then said:

"Also please help the people who have been appointed by the Church to follow up on your appearances in Rwanda, they need your help. You see, I don't work with them, they only ask me questions. But when I think about it and when I hear what people say about it outside, I think they have a really hard job that needs wisdom and intelligence to do it. Sometimes work can be overwhelming, please help them as you know how it is when somebody is tired, but with your help they can do things right despite how weary they are. Please help them to know that they are working for you, and for God and for the Church. Help them to feel passion and eagerness to bring justice to the whole situation. I mean, they need strength, especially since they have other work to do as well. Please give them the necessary strength."

The visionaries went through a lot during those investigations, a lot of pain, but Alphonsine is still praying for those who are doing the investigations, especially that they can do a good job and the truth can be made clear. How many times do we pray for our bosses and their work or those in authority especially when we are not appreciating how they treat us? Let us pray we have the strength to do this for love of neighbor.

She listened and then spoke referring to another person, a man or woman whom we didn't know:

"I know it was really hard for him/her, really hard. You see and he/she is a bit old, which doesn't make it easier either, even if he/she is old physically, he/she is definitely strong in his/her words, but he/she needs strength. You know a person is a person, we are weak. Sometimes difficulties come and it is possible to bear it. At other times, it can be unbearable, especially when you don't have somebody who can help you to deal with them and to share the pain with. You see all the problems he/she went through these days, please help him/her. I haven't asked him/her about that."

She listened and then said:

"He/she wanted to tell me about that, but I couldn't stay. I was running and we couldn't talk about it that well. But since you normally communicate to him/her what you think, I think you should do the same again. I don't know how you want to do it, but he/she is not too sure. He/she is still confused about which way to take, and especially with all he/she saw."

She listened and said:

"Yes, if you don't come to his/her help, he/she will get discouraged. You know how it is when you try to do good for people, and you try your best and no one notices it, except a good friend who knows you well, you get tired quickly. For example, if I take myself for instance and if I try to do good to people I live with and I try to please them and see that they don't see it, and sometimes lose sleep because of them or don't even eat on time because I am trying to do what is good for them, and no one sees your efforts, it really gets discouraging and you wish at least they would see your efforts. Please come to his/her help and you know many times he/she trusted

in you. You know I don't have to say much. When people say bad things about you, you can't go and tell them that they are lying. It is impossible. You just pray no matter how much it hurts."

She listened and then said:

"I saw he/she can take it. I see that he/she doesn't have any problem with this at all. You know the truth hurts to some people, for example, when somebody says what they have done after so much work to get to what they wanted to do, there are some people who will never believe how hard that person has worked, some try to destroy what another has done, or call it lies when it is true. But somehow, I find him/her strong, and he/she lives with a good family, good people. It wouldn't be too much of a problem, especially that he/she has another job, and for me I saw that what he/she did was purely to try to show what was right. I haven't told him/her everything yet, I thought it was not necessary, you see, I don't talk to him/her much, I didn't want to tell him/her so as not to add to his/her worries, even if I think he/she is strong enough to take it. I think he/she did it because he/she thought it was the right thing to do and it was his/her responsibility, especially that he/she has started the whole thing. I will tell him/her because you now told me to do so, but in the first place, I thought it wasn't necessary, now I see he/she can take it."

As I said earlier, in the Rwandan native language, which this message was given in, the language is such that you don't know exactly who the person is she is talking about. We cannot know if it is a man or a woman, unless they mention the name or they say who it is. Alphonsine kept referring to some people in the third person so we don't know who they are. This allowed for the person to remain anonymous to the public, for that knowledge was meant to be shared only between Alphonsine and Our Lady.

She listened and then said:

"*I can see him/her tomorrow, there is no problem.*"

She listened for a while as she said:

"*Yes.*"

And sometimes:

"*No.*"

And then said:

"*I offer you my family, my brothers and all the problems they have.*"

She listened and then said to those who were there:

"*My children, I always listen to you, but in a special way, since you have traveled from so far away to come here, in this moment, I am asking you to take a silent moment and from the bottom of your heart, tell me what is in your heart.*"

Everyone took a little time to address themselves to Our Lady, in silence to say what they needed, and then Alphonsine said:

"*My dear Mother Virgin Mary, I beg you to come to the help all those who pray.*"

She listened for a while and then started to sing:

"*We run to you because we are in a place of a lot of tears. Our advocate, please take care of us and have mercy on us and when we leave this earth, please guide us to your Son Jesus. You are a Mother worthy of all our respect."*

She listened for a while and then she repeated what she was told to say:

"My children, I am going to say goodbye to you. I love you, I love you, I love you. But woe to the one who will ignore the love I promise you and which I reveal to you. I came for you, I came for you, I came for you, because I saw that you needed me."

Alphonsine then spoke with a deep sadness in her voice and her eyes filled with tears as she said:

"I thank you so much my dear mother. I beg you to be near me always."

In response to what was told her she said:

"I told you all I had to tell you. I thank you for explaining a lot of what I couldn't understand and what you hadn't explained to me before. I am sure I will continue to understand much more over time all those things you have told me. I beg you to be near me always."

Then she started to sing:

"You see what my future will become Mary, because of the voice of God. Come and strengthen me, Maria. Give me patience and discretion. You see what my future will become, Mary, because of the voice of God. I have packed all that belongs to me, and I came to you and put all in your hands, Mary. Be loved, you who deserve to be loved, Maria. Be thanked, you who deserve to be thanked, Mary."

Some songs in Kibeho were taught by Our Lady herself and this was believed to be one of them. Other songs you see throughout the apparitions were sung and written by other people, and many times Our Lady singles out the ones she loves and asks the visionary to sing it. It is the culture of Rwanda to sing in families, especially at night, during Igitaramo, which is a family gathering after dinner before going to sleep where family members will sing or even dance together. It always brought the whole family together, even the extended family. Most of the time, the grandparents lived nearby as well as uncles and aunts and they too would come to join in as one family where we would often times meet in the courtyard. Our Lady respected our culture and many times she would request a few songs for everyone to dance to at the end of the apparition.

She then said:

"I thank you very much. I will continue to think of my life, who I was, how I was born. I still don't understand why God chose me. I will continue to reflect on the love with which you loved me by allowing me to see you with my own eyes, knowing well that I don't deserve it. Even the things we just spoke about, I feel like I don't deserve any of it. Help me to keep all that in my heart always. I will not betray you. I offer you all the Christians from everywhere in the world. Thank you very much."

With a lot of tears, Alphonsine started to sing the Magnificat in Kinyarwanda with a heaviness and great sadness in her voice, which was so apparent as her voice was faintly heard. As she was singing she fell down in the middle of the song and you could hear her singing which she couldn't continue after two lines:

"My soul proclaims the greatness of the Lord, and my spirit rejoices in God my savior, for He has looked with mercy on His…."

The apparition ended at 5:30 p.m. Those who were there left in sadness as well.

This message was for you and for me. Our Lady once said, "*If I am coming to Rwanda it doesn't mean that I am concerned only for the diocese of Butare, or for Rwanda, or for whole of Africa, I am concerned with and coming for the whole world.*" I hope you enjoy these messages as much as I do. Let's pray for one another and remember that we are called to live and spread Our Lady's messages with great love.

Alphonsine after the apparition falling, half way to the ground.

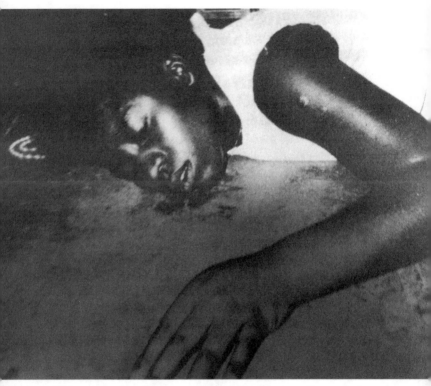

Alphonsine after the apparition fell like a tree to the ground, sometimes to a bare cement floor."

Messages To Remember

1. Our Lady loves the Rosary. It is a very powerful prayer and she wants us to pray it daily.

2. Our Lady wants people to love her as their mother and to encourage others to love her.

3. Our Lady promises us that if we pray and follow the Bible and the Gospel of her Son, we will ALWAYS have peace in our hearts.

4. Our Lady reminds us that a good heart surpasses all; there are no riches that are beyond a clean heart.

5. Our Lady loves songs that have good messages.

6. Our Mother wants us to talk to her and tell her all that troubles our hearts.

7. Our Lady wants us to pray for the Church and Church Leaders.

8. Our Lady wants us to pray for one another; we are in this world together and sharing the same journey.

9. Our Lady loves you and she warns you not to forget the love she promises you.

10. Our Lady wants us to go to confession often. She once mentioned that she would like us to go at least once a month, but you can go as often as you like. Pope John Paul II went every day!

11. Our Lady reminds us to be thankful even for our troubles. If we live without problems, we will never learn the lessons that we learn through resolving those problems.

12. Our Lady reminds us that we should care for each other enough to kindly and prudently correct one another if we do wrong.

13. Our Lady reminds us that the child of Mary always bears crosses graciously. The child of Mary dies with many words in the heart. The child of Mary carries crosses with joy. The child of Mary sees the world as nothing.

14. Our Lady tells us that every good Christian can be God's messenger.

Alphonsine's Inspirational Words

1. **Alphonsine:** "…I think about everything and I think it was necessary, even if I suffered a lot on the way. You know how people are. We are proud, we don't like to get our feelings hurt, but I think it was necessary for me to go through it. All I had to suffer, I now understand that it was necessary for me to go through it to know the truth, and learn more about life…"

2. **Alphonsine:** "…You told me that the people in general are afraid of suffering. We love that nothing makes us suffer at all, but as you repeated to me many times, crosses teach us a lot as we become smarter, wiser. It also gives each one of us an occasion to increase our love for God by showing Him that you can still do something for God, even when you are suffering like this…"

3. **Alphonsine:** "…I have been watching, you see we try to see the wrong in people instead of trying to see what is good. When people do good, we try to hide it, when they do wrong, we publicize it. I hope you come to our help because you know our problems…"

4. **Alphonsine:** "…It is only you who can make a difference in that situation. I will continue to pray about it. Since you spoke about people of every walk of life, as Christians we will be praying for everybody, we will be praying for children, our leaders, for families and for those who

dedicated their lives to God. To hear the messages is one thing, but to put them into practice is another thing. It is not easy...."

5. **Alphonsine:** "...Give me grace to love the poor, those who have nobody, and those who don't have anyone to understand them. Give me true kindness, the grace to live good with others. Give me humility, so that those who will come to me will find a welcoming soul so they don't get scared if it depends on how I behave towards them. Give me the grace to love prayer always. Give me the grace to teach others how to pray. Grant me the grace to forgive because I wouldn't live with anyone if I couldn't forgive, as we all make mistakes. Give me the grace to share the good I have. Don't let me be overfed when there is a hungry person at my door. Give me the grace so I won't close the door to the hungry. Please help me not to tell anyone that I don't have time, especially when what they need of me is important to their soul. In a few words, please help me to live like a good Christian, as God wants me to..."

6. **Alphonsine:** "...But I am asking you, Mother, to give me strength to accomplish all you need of me, until my death. I am begging you to help me to be a good model everywhere I go or live, so that I won't be a reason for anyone to fall. I am asking you for help to save souls. I am asking you to help me to be a reason for joy in a good way, for those I will meet in my life. Please give me the grace to receive with kindness all those who will be coming to me, especially those who would like to know you through me. Grant that I may never complain about my work. Give me strength not to be tired and if I am, grant me patience.

Give me the wisdom to know when I need to rest and rest only when I need to..."

7. **Alphonsine:** "...Please help me so that wherever I will go people won't think of me as God or Mary, that they will see me as your instrument who was here only to deliver your message. Help them to remember that even someone who sees something special in me will recognize that they too can be your messengers in their own ways, that every good Christian can be God's messenger. Help me to be treated like everyone else for I know that whenever I go by people they may refer to me as the one who had an apparition, and point fingers at me. That is okay, but Mother help me, so when I make friends or acquaintances and we are talking, they will not hold themselves back, but be free to be themselves or tell me whatever they want because they might remember that they are talking to the one who has seen you. I ask for your help so that people will not love me only during the time of their need of prayer. As I myself have lived that before, please, if possible, go into their hearts and change them from within. I can pray, but only you can change their hearts so that they will see me as a normal person..."

Our Lady's Words

1. **Our Lady:** "My children, pray, pray, follow the Bible and the Gospel of my Son so you will always have peace in your heart. My Son suffered so much, He was humiliated, He was persecuted, but He still is the King of Heaven and Earth."

2. **Our Lady:** "You all who are called crazy because you like to pray, all of you who are called thieves, those to whom they say that you are losing time by giving your life to God, I tell you one day you will be happy."

3. **Our Lady:** "My children, I give you my blessing. I am not giving it only to those who are here in Kibeho, but also to those in the world."

4. **Our Lady:** "All of you who are sick with incurable sicknesses, a good heart surpasses all, there are no riches that are beyond a clean heart. All of you who have had difficulties of all kinds, there are difficulties everywhere, in all walks of life. When they don't go away, offer them to God. Every good Christian is requested to offer a sacrifice. All of you who have problems in your families, think of the Holy Family, who lived in such poverty, and who lived among those who didn't like them nor understand them, and with the problems you have, come close to them. All of you who have dedicated your lives to God, a life like that is not easy. The most important thing is to be faithful to your promises. All of you young people, when you are young, you think that you can do anything; be careful not to fall

and damage yourself for good. All of you leaders, who have the capacity to represent many people, don't kill, but save; don't be greedy, but share with others, and don't attempt to hurt those who are trying to expose your wrongdoings. I tell you, anyone you want to hurt, because they love people and are defending human rights, because they are defending the cause of the poor and the simple, because they are defending anything good and trying to love God, I tell you, whatever you do will be in vain."

5. **Our Lady:** "My children, saying goodbye to you doesn't mean that I am forgetting Africa, not even the whole world. It doesn't mean that I am going to forget Rwandans. Alphonsine was my instrument, she is not your God. I am asking you not to forget the love I have loved you with when I came to your country. I am asking you not to forget the trips you have made to Rwanda."

6. **Our Lady:** "My children, in truth, I am not staying as long as I used to do as I have told you all that was necessary. I have just told you what more I needed from you. As I said, I want to remind you that I am happy. I am happy with the fruits that were born in Rwanda since I came here. Don't worry about the difficulties you have. Nothing is better than having God. My dear children, problems exist everywhere, but the most important thing is to have an accepting heart without complaining.

7. **Our Lady:** "My children, I am going to say goodbye to you. I love you, I love you, I love you. But woe to the one who will ignore the love I promise you and which I reveal to you. I came for you, I came for you, I came for you, because I saw that you needed me."

Prayer To Our Lady of Kibeho

Blessed Virgin Mary, Mother of the Word, Mother of all those who believe in Him and who welcome Him into their lives, we are here before you to contemplate you. We believe that you are amongst us, like a mother in the midst of her children, even though we do not see you with our bodily eyes.

We bless you, the sure way that leads us to Jesus the Savior, for all the favors which you endlessly pour out upon us, especially that, in your meekness, you were gracious enough to appear miraculously in Kibeho, just when our world needed it most.

Grant us always the light and the strength necessary to accept, with all seriousness, your call to us to be converted, to repent, and to live according to your Son's Gospel. Teach us how to pray with sincerity, and to love one another as He loved us, so that, just as you have requested, we may always be beautiful flowers diffusing their pleasant fragrance everywhere and upon everyone.

Holy Mary, Our Lady of Sorrows, teach us to understand the value of the cross in our lives, so that whatever is still lacking to the sufferings of Christ we may fill up in our own bodies for His mystical Body, which is the Church.

And, when our pilgrimage on this earth comes to an end, may we live eternally with you in the kingdom of Heaven.

Amen.

Imprimatur: Gikongoro, the 25th of March, 2006

+August Misago-Bishop of Gikongoro

The Rosary of the Seven Sorrows of the Virgin Mary

This rosary recalls the seven major sorrows that the Virgin Mary suffered through—albeit with love and compassion—during the life, trials, and agonizing death of her son, Jesus Christ. It's very special to the immaculate heart of the Blessed mother, and she wants all of us to say it as often as possible.

The Rosary of the seven sorrows dates back to the middle ages, but it gained new popularity following the Marian apparitions in Kibeho, which have been approved by the catholic church. During Mary's apparitions to Marie-Claire Mukangango, she assigned the young visionary a mission to reintroduce this special rosary to the world. Before her untimely death, Marie-Claire did just that, traveling widely to teach it to thousands of people, who then taught it to thousands of others.

During her visitations to Kibeho, the Holy Virgin revealed that this rosary possesses immense spiritual power for those who say it sincerely. She promised that when prayed with an open and repentant heart, the rosary would win us the Lord's forgiveness for our sins and free our souls from guilt and remorse.

She also promised that over time, the rosary would develop within us a deep understanding of why we sin, and that knowledge would give us the wisdom and strength to change or remove any internal flaws, weaknesses of character, or personality faults causing unhappiness and keeping us from enjoying the joyous life god intended for us to live.

The Rosary of the seven sorrows contains all the power you need to change your life for the better, obtain peace and happiness, realize your true potential, fulfill all your dreams, and grow closer to god's light. During one of her many apparitions to Marie-Claire, the Holy Virgin suggested that it be prayed as often as possible, but especially on Tuesdays and Fridays: Tuesday being the day Mary first appeared to Marie-Claire, and Friday being the day Christ was crucified. The Blessed mother also stressed that the Rosary of the seven sorrows is intended to complement—and in no way replace—the traditional rosary. Pray both rosaries regularly and you'll be doubly blessed!

The third visionary, Marie Claire, during the apparition.
She was given the mission to teach the Seven Sorrows Rosary to the world.
She was killed during the genocide.

How to Pray
The Rosary of the Seven
Sorrows of the Virgin Mary

The following is a description of this amazing rosary as the Virgin mother herself taught it to Marie-Claire in Kibeho. It may be prayed aloud or contemplated silently, alone or with others; the key is for the prayers, reflections, and meditations to always come from the depths of your heart.

I speak from experience when I promise that you'll never regret learning this wonderful rosary and that you'll soon lose track of the countless blessings that praying it will bring into your life. It's my hope that more people than ever before will learn just how amazing this rosary is.

Please note that you don't necessarily need any special beads to say these prayers; just follow the diagram and instructions on the following page. (It is, however, important that when you reach each sorrowful mystery, you take a moment to meditate on the magnitude of Mary's suffering . . . and the strength of her love.)

1. On the large medal at the bottom of the rosary:
   a. Make the sign of the cross.
   b. Say the Introductory Prayer.
   c. Say the act of contrition.

2. For each of the next three beads, say a Hail Mary.

3. On the first small medal:
   a. Say the prayer, "most merciful mother, remind us always about the sorrows of your son, Jesus."
   b. Meditate upon the first sorrowful mystery.
   c. Say the Lord's Prayer.

4. For each of the next seven beads, say a Hail Mary.

5. On the second small medal:
   a. Say the prayer, "Most merciful mother . . ."
   b. Meditate upon the second sorrowful mystery.
   c. Say the Lord's Prayer.

6. For each of the next seven beads, say a Hail Mary.

7. On the third small medal:
   a. Say the prayer, "Most merciful mother . . ."
   b. Meditate upon the third sorrowful mystery.
   c. Say the Lord's Prayer.

8. For each of the next seven beads, say a Hail Mary.

9. On the fourth small medal:
   a. Say the prayer, "most merciful mother . . ."
   b. Meditate upon the fourth sorrowful mystery.
   c. Say the Lord's Prayer.

10. For each of the next seven beads, say a Hail Mary.

11. On the fifth small medal:
    a. Say the prayer, "most merciful mother . . ."
    b. Meditate upon the fifth sorrowful mystery.
    c. Say the Lord's Prayer.

12. For each of the next seven beads, say a Hail Mary.

13. On the sixth small medal:
    a. say the prayer, "most merciful mother . . ."
    b. Meditate upon the sixth sorrowful mystery.
    c. Say the Lord's Prayer.

14. For each of the next seven beads, say a Hail Mary.

15. On the seventh small medal:
    a. Say the prayer, "most merciful mother . . ."
    b. Meditate upon the seventh sorrowful mystery.
    c. Say the Lord's Prayer.

16. For each of the next seven beads, say a Hail Mary.

17. Upon reaching the large medal at the bottom of the rosary:
    a. Say the prayer, "most merciful mother . . ."
    b. Say the concluding Prayer.
    c. Say three times: "Mary, who was conceived without sin and who suffered for us, pray for us."

Make a sign of the cross; your prayers will be answered!

— **Introductory Prayer:** *My God, I offer You this rosary for Your glory, so I may honor Your Holy Mother, the Blessed Virgin, so I can share and meditate upon her suffering. I humbly beg You to give me true repentance for all my sins. Give me wisdom and humility so that I may receive all the indulgences contained in this prayer.*

— **Act of Contrition:** *O my God, I am heartily sorry for having offended You, and I detest all my sins because I dread the loss of heaven and the pains of hell; but most of all because they offend You, my God, You Who are all good and deserving of all my love. I firmly resolve, with the help of Your grace, to confess my sins, to do penance, and to amend my life. Amen.*

— **Before Each Mystery, Pray:** *Most merciful mother, remind us always about the sorrows of your son, Jesus.*

1. The First Sorrowful Mystery: The Prophecy of Simeon (Luke 2:22–35)

The Blessed Virgin Mary took Jesus to the temple, as tradition demanded that all newborns be blessed in the temple before god. There, the old priest Simeon held the baby Jesus in his hands, and the Holy spirit filled his heart. Simeon recognized Jesus as the promised savior and held the child high toward heaven, thanking god for granting his wish that he would live long enough to behold the Messiah.

"Now your servant may depart this life in peace, my Lord," he said. Then he looked upon Mary and proclaimed, "and you, woman, a sword of sorrow will pierce your heart because of the suffering that shall befall your child."

The Blessed Virgin knew that she had given birth to the savior of humankind, so she immediately understood and accepted Simeon's prophecy. Although her heart was deeply touched by this favor of bearing the baby Jesus, her heart remained heavy and troubled, for she knew what had been written about the ordeals and subsequent death of the savior. Whenever she saw her son, she was constantly reminded of the suffering he would be subjected to, and his suffering became her own.

Prayer: *Beloved Mother Mary, whose heart suffered beyond bearing because of us, teach us to suffer with you and with love, and to accept all the suffering God deems it necessary to send our way. Let us suffer, and may our suffering be known to God only, like yours and that of Jesus. Do not let us show our suffering to the world, so it will matter more and be used to atone for the sins of the world. You, Mother, who suffered with the Savior of the world, we offer you our suffering, and the suffering of the world, because we are your children. Join those sorrows to your own and to those of the Lord Jesus Christ, then offer them to God the Father so that He will know the one who created it. You are a mother greater than all.*

2. The Second Sorrowful Mystery: The Flight into Egypt (Matthew 2:13–15)

Mary's heart broke and her mind was greatly troubled when Joseph revealed to her the words of the angel: they were to wake up quickly and flee to Egypt because Herod wanted to kill Jesus. The Blessed Virgin hardly had time to decide what to take or leave behind; she took her child and left everything else, rushing outside before Joseph so that they could hurry as god wished. Then she said, "even though god has power over everything, He wants us to flee with Jesus, His son. God will show us the way, and we shall arrive without being caught by the enemy."

Because the Blessed Virgin was the mother of Jesus, she loved him more than anyone else. Her heart was deeply troubled at the sight of her infant son's discomfort, and she suffered greatly because he was cold and shivering. While she and her husband were tired, sleepy, and hungry during this long travel, Mary's only thought was about the safety and comfort of her child. She feared coming face-to-face with the soldiers who had been ordered to kill Jesus because she was aware that the enemy was still in Bethlehem. Her heart remained constantly anguished during this flight. She also knew that where they were going, there would be no friendly faces to greet them.

Prayer: *Beloved Mother, who has suffered so much, give to us your courageous heart. Give us strength so that we can be brave like you and accept with love the suffering God sends our way. Help us to also accept all the suffering we inflict upon ourselves and the suffering inflicted upon us by others. Heavenly Mother, you alone purify our suffering so that we may give glory to God and save our souls.*

3. The Third Sorrowful Mystery: The Loss of Jesus in the Temple (Luke 2:41–52)

Jesus was the only begotten son of god, but he was also Mary's child. The Blessed Virgin loved Jesus more than herself because he was her god. Compared to other children, he was most unique because he was already living as god. When Mary lost Jesus on their way back from Jerusalem, the world became so big and lonely that she believed she couldn't go on living without him, so great was her sorrow. (She felt the same pain her son felt when he was later abandoned by his apostles during the Passion.)

As the Holy mother looked anxiously for her beloved boy, deep pain welled in her heart. She blamed herself, asking why she didn't take greater care of him. But it was not her fault; Jesus no longer needed her protection as before. What really hurt Mary was that her son had decided to stay behind without her consent. Jesus had pleased her in everything so far: He never annoyed her in any way, nor would he ever displease his parents. She knew that he always did what was necessary, however, so she never suspected him of being disobedient.

Prayer: *Beloved Mother, teach us to accept all our sufferings because of our sins and to atone for the sins of the whole world.*

4. The Fourth Sorrowful Mystery: Mary Meets Jesus on the Way to Calvary (Luke 23:27–31)

Mary witnessed Jesus carrying the heavy cross alone—the cross on which he was to be crucified. This didn't surprise the Blessed Virgin because she already knew about the approaching death of Our Lord. Noting how her son was already weakened by the numerous hard blows given by the soldiers' clubs, she was filled with anguish at his pain.

The soldiers kept hurrying and pushing him, though he had no strength left. He fell, exhausted, unable to raise himself. At that moment, Mary's eyes, so full of tender love and compassion, met her son's eyes, which were pained and covered in blood. Their hearts seemed to be sharing the load; every pain he felt, she felt as well. They knew that nothing could be done except to believe and trust in god and dedicate their suffering to Him. All they could do was put everything in god's hands.

Prayer: *Beloved Mother, so stricken with grief, help us to bear our own suffering with courage and love so that we may relieve your sorrowful heart and that of Jesus. In doing so, may we give glory to God Who gave you and Jesus to humanity. As you suffered, teach us to suffer silently and patiently. Grant unto us the grace of loving God in everything. O Mother of Sorrows, most afflicted of all mothers, have mercy on the sinners of the whole world.*

5. The Fifth Sorrowful Mystery: Mary Stands at the Foot of the Cross (John 19:25–27)

The Blessed Virgin Mary continued to climb the mount to calvary, following behind Jesus painfully and sorrowfully, yet suffering silently. She could see him staggering and falling with the cross some more, and she witnessed her son being beaten by soldiers who pulled his hair to force him to stand up.

Despite his innocence, when Jesus reached the top of calvary, he was ordered to confess in front of the crowd so they could laugh at him. Mary deeply felt her son's pain and humiliation, particularly when his tormentors forced him to strip off what was left of his clothing. The Blessed Virgin felt sick at heart seeing these tyrants crucifying her son naked, shaming him terribly merely to amuse the jeering crowd. (Jesus and Mary felt more disgrace than normal people did because they were holy and without sin.)

The Blessed Virgin Mary felt pain beyond bearing when Jesus was stretched out on the cross. His murderers sang merrily as they approached him with hammers and nails. They sat on him heavily so that he could not move when they spiked him to the wood. As they hammered the nails through his hands and feet, Mary felt the blows in her heart; the nails pierced her flesh as they tore into her son's body. She felt her life fading away.

As the soldiers lifted the cross to drop it into the hole they'd dug, they deliberately jerked it, causing the force of Jesus's bodily weight to tear through the flesh on his hands and expose his bone. The pain shot through his body like liquid fire. He endured three excruciating hours skewered on the cross, yet the physical pain was nothing compared to the agonizing heartache he was forced to bear seeing his mother suffering below him. Mercifully, he finally died.

Prayer: *Beloved Mother, Queen of the Martyrs, give us the courage you had in all your sufferings so that we may unite our sufferings with yours and give glory to God. Help us follow all His commandments and those of the Church so that Our Lord's sacrifice will not be in vain, and all sinners in the world will be saved.*

6. The Sixth Sorrowful Mystery: Mary Receives the Dead Body of Jesus in Her Arms (John 19:38–40)

The friends of Jesus, Joseph and Nicodemus, took down his body from the cross and placed it in the outstretched arms of the Blessed Virgin. Then Mary washed it with deep respect and love because she was his mother. She knew better than anyone else that he was god incarnate who'd taken a human body to become the savior of all people.

Mary could see the terrifying wounds from the flogging Jesus had received while at Pilate's. His flesh had been shredded and large strips had been torn from his back. His entire body had been so lacerated that gaping wounds crisscrossed him from head to toe. Mary found that the wounds from the nails were less severe than those caused by the flogging and by carrying the cross. She was horrified at the thought that her son had managed to carry the heavy, splintered cross all the way to calvary. She saw the circle of blood the crown of thorns had made on his forehead and, to her horror, realized that many of the barbed thorns had dug so deeply into his skull they had penetrated his brain.

Looking at her broken boy, the Holy mother knew that his agonizing death was far worse than the torture reserved for the wickedest of criminals. As she cleaned his damaged body, she envisioned him during each stage of his short life, remembering her first look at his beautiful newborn face as the two of them lay in the manger, and every day in between, until this heartrending moment as she gently bathed his lifeless body. Her anguish was relentless as she prepared her son and Lord for burial, but she remained brave and strong, becoming the true Queen of martyrs. As she washed her son, she prayed that everybody would know the riches of paradise and enter the gates of heaven. She prayed for every soul in the world to embrace god's love so her son's torturous death would benefit all humankind and would not have been in vain. Mary prayed for the world; she prayed for all of us.

Prayer: *We thank you, Beloved Mother, for your courage as you stood beneath your dying child to comfort him on the cross. As our Savior drew his last breath, you became a wonderful mother to all of us; you became the Blessed Mother of the world. We know that you love us more than our own earthly parents do. We implore you to be our advocate before the throne of mercy and grace so that we can truly become your children. We thank you for Jesus, our Savior and Redeemer, and we thank Jesus for giving you to us. Please pray for us, Mother.*

7. The Seventh Sorrowful Mystery: Jesus Is Placed in the Tomb (John 19:41–42)

The life of the Blessed Virgin Mary was so closely linked to that of Jesus she thought there was no reason for her to go on living any longer. Her only comfort was that his death had ended his unspeakable suffering. Our sorrowful mother, with the help of John and the holy women, devoutly placed Jesus's body in the sepulchre, and she left him there as any other dead person. She went home with great pain and tremendous sorrow; for the first time she was without him, and her loneliness was a new and bitter source of pain. Her heart had been dying since her son's heart had stopped beating, but she was certain that our savior would soon be resurrected.

Prayer: *Most Beloved Mother, whose beauty surpassed that of all mothers, mother of mercy, mother of Jesus, and mother to us all, we are your children and we place all our trust in you. Teach us to see God in all things and all situations, even in our sufferings. Help us to understand the importance of suffering, and also to know the purpose of our suffering as God had intended it.*

You yourself were conceived and born without sin, were preserved from sin, yet you suffered more than anybody else has. You accepted suffering and pain with love and with unsurpassed courage. You stood by your son from the time he was arrested until he died. You suffered along with him, felt every pain and torment he did. You accomplished the will of God the Father; and according to His will, you have become our savior with Jesus. We beg you, dear Mother, to teach us to do as Jesus did. Teach us to accept our cross courageously. We trust you, most merciful mother, so teach us to sacrifice for all the sinners in the world. Help us to follow in your son's footsteps, and even to be willing to lay down our lives for others.

— Concluding Prayer: *Queen of Martyrs, your heart suffered so much. I beg you, by the merits of the tears you shed in these terrible and sorrowful times, to obtain for me and all the sinners of the world the grace of complete sincerity and repentance. Amen. Three times, say: Mary, who was conceived without sin and who suffered for us, pray for us.*

Congratulations on finishing the Rosary of the seven sorrows of the Virgin Mary! Now make the sign of the cross to wipe away the tears Mary shed during the Passion of Jesus, and rest assured that your prayers will be answered!

Acknowledgments

To my Dear Father God Almighty who makes all things possible, I thank you with all my heart for the gift of Our Lady and for allowing this book to be. I pray that the effort of this book, through these unworthy hands, will make You proud. My infinite gratitude goes to my Mother Mary for all the blessings you entrusted Kibeho, and my home country of Rwanda, to share with the world. Also with all my heart, I am so thankful to you Alphonsine Mumureke for being a beautiful instrument and for your words and prayers that inspire us. Also, my gratitude goes to my fellow Apostles of Our Lady of Kibeho around the world who have wished this book to be and who have helped me in shaping it, providing information, editing and pictures. My heart goes out to you all. We are on this journey together and thank you for holding my hands along the way. I will thank God forever for bringing you into my life: the groups of The Flowers of Our Lady of Kibeho in Rwanda, the Apostles of Our Lady in Australia, and the team of My Saint My Hero in California.

To Greg Jamaya, Christine Rich and Christopher Ashton for helping edit this book, you were a gift from heaven. To my dearest Kathy Lesnar for all your love and your support you give me and you give to this work and for joining your efforts to mine in spreading Our Lady's messages. I am forever grateful to God for bringing you into my life. To you my dear friend and brother, Michael Collapy, thank you for your kindness and for being a great photographer. I couldn't do this book without the love and inspiration from my family and friends, especially the kids, Nikki, BJ, Aaryana, Ryan, Loanna, Logan and the littlest Keziah, the newest addition to the family. You make it possible to wake up in the morning and dream about tomorrow with a smile because you are so, so, good!

A church that became a memorial of the genocide after 1994. There are thousands of remains of people who were killed there. This is what Our Lady tried to prevent, the genocide. Her statue remains standing there covered by dust in sadness watching over the bodies of her children.

Kibeho today, I go there with pilgrims from around the world to celebrate the very first visit of Our Lady every November 28. This was the Feast of 2009, there was a multitude of people praying, dancing and singing and thanking God for sending Mary to visit us.

People camp around the shrine in Kibeho for days and weeks to wait for the celebration on November 28. They do it to pray, and prepare their hearts for this important day. Thousands come on foot and travel for days to pray even longer and prepare themselves.

Blessings are given every November 28 and people bring gallons of water to be blessed and go back to bless those they left home.

First pilgrimage to Kibeho March 2009 at CANA center in Kibeho.

Pilgrimage July 2009 in Kibeho.

Pilgrimage November 2009 with visionary Anathalie in white at the shrine. It is always a joy for me to share Kibeho with the pilgrims!

OUR LADY OF KIBEHO RETREAT WITH IMMACULÉE
SAN PEDRO, CALIFORNIA

Today conferences and retreats are held around the world to honor and learn about our Lady of Kibeho. This was a photo taken during a retreat I gave in New Orleans in 2010."

Apostles of Our Lady of Kibeho in the USA raised money to build an elementary school in Kibeho! Kate Lesnar (15 years old) with the help of her sister Annnie Lesnar (13 years old) played golf all day for Africa and raised $10,000 to buy the water tank for the school in July 2010.